Wiltsh

PLACE-NAMES

THEIR ORIGINS AND MEANINGS

Martyn Whittock

COUNTRYSIDE BOOKS
NEWBURY, BERKSHIRE

First published 1997
© Martyn Whittock 1997

COUNTRYSIDE BOOKS
3 Catherine Road
Newbury, Berkshire

ISBN 1 85306 486 6

*For Simon, Charlotte, Tilly and Toby Bruce,
with thanks for their friendship*

Cover photo supplied by Roger Holman
Illustrations by Muriel Hodgson
Map by Trevor Yorke

Produced through MRM Associates Ltd., Reading
Printed by J. W. Arrowsmith Ltd., Bristol

INTRODUCTION

The aim of this book is to provide the general reader with an opportunity to explore and unpackage the rich heritage of Wiltshire's place-names. This is particularly important as most other works on the subject are long out of print, such as *The Place-names of Wiltshire*, by E. Ekblom (1917), *Notes on Wiltshire Place-names*, by J.C. Longstaff (1911), and *Wiltshire Place-names*, by R. Tomkins (1983). *The Place-names of Wiltshire* (1939), published by the English Place-Names Society, is arguably far more detailed, expensive and complex than that required by the general reader. Also it is organised according to Hundreds, the ancient subdivisions of the county which group parishes together rather than alphabetically by place.

This present guide is deeply indebted to these earlier works but aims to be more 'user friendly' to the general reader than the more complex of them, while taking note of the latest research by place-names scholars such as Dr Margaret Gelling. As such it offers readers an easily approached route to essential information about a very wide selection of Wiltshire place-names, without overwhelming them with unnecessary detail and complexity of layout.

All entries in this guide are organised alphabetically, with their meaning and where relevant an overview of how their spelling has changed with time. Other names within the area of each larger settlement are then explored including names of streets, nearby smaller settlements and landscape features. To gain a flavour of the history of settlements other pieces of relevant historical information are often included.

Wiltshire is a county of striking geography. In the north the claylands of the north Wiltshire plain run into Oxfordshire and the Thames valley. To the north-west the limestone hills are cut by the sweeping curves of the Bristol Avon, flowing towards the Severn sea. But the heart of the county is dominated by the wide open horizons and rolling downland of the high chalk. North of the Vale of Pewsey and the valley of the river Kennet, the Marlborough Downs roll north and east to join the Berkshire Downs, whilst south of Pewsey the wild, high expanse of Salisbury plain hangs like a great crescent, whose western arm becomes part of Cranborne Chase, south of the river Nadder, and runs into Dorset. West of this curve of chalk the claylands of the Vale of Wardour, the upper Avon and around Trowbridge separate the chalk from the limestone.

Lying at the heart of central, southern England the high dry land of Wiltshire has provided access across the region since the New Stone Age. Countless generations have left their mark on the archaeology of the county and later on its rich variety of place-names, which record the sites of their farms, hamlets, villages and towns. The medieval wealth of the county's downland sheep is reflected in magnificent urban centres such as Salisbury and in the names of the medieval manorial lords who exploited its wealth and who are recorded in so many place-names.

Wiltshire itself is a creation of the Anglo-Saxons and was one of the areas of local government – the shires – established before the Norman Conquest. The name, in the form **Wilsaetan** ('the settlers on the river Wylye'), is first recorded in the *Anglo-Saxon Chronicle* for the year AD 800. Its more familiar form **Wiltunscir** ('the shire centred on Wilton') is mentioned in AD 870. The modern county name has developed from this.

The county map is scattered with over 2,000 years of place-names. By unlocking their meaning it is possible to explore some of the most intriguing and stimulating aspects of local history. Here lies recorded much of the history of the settlement and exploitation of the resources of the county which frequently does not exist in any other form. At times it can be used to correct, or complement, evidence from other sources such as archaeology and written documents.

However, there are few areas of interest where the pitfalls are as big as the possibilities. This is because the meanings of most place-names are hidden by changes in language over centuries. **Slaughterford**, northwest of Corsham, sounds like the site of some ancient battle; however, the Tax Record of 1291 records that its name was **Slahtreford** – 'the ford of the Sloetrees, or Blackthorns'. To solve the clues it is therefore necessary to unlock the ancient languages from which most modern place-names were originally formed. The earliest recorded forms of each place-name need careful scrutiny.

The vast majority of modern Wiltshire place-names were formed between the 5th and 11th centuries AD. They are products of Anglo-Saxon England. The language spoken in this period was Old English, for simplicity described here as Saxon which, with the addition of many other 'ingredients' is the ancestor of Modern English. There are important similarities between Saxon and Modern English. For example, the ancient word which gave rise to the 'ford' in **Codford**, on the river Wylye, has not changed in its meaning, or appearance, in over 1,000 years. Other words though have undergone significant changes. The 'cod' part of Codford has nothing to do with fish, but comes from the probable Saxon personal-name Codda. Modern place-names frequently contain elements which are no longer self-explanatory.

Had there been no Anglo-Saxon settlement in the Dark Ages, the inhabitants of Wiltshire would now be speaking a form of Welsh. The ancestor of the Modern Welsh language – British, which developed into Primitive Welsh during the Dark Ages – was the language of what is now England at the time of the Anglo-Saxon settlement. Some place-names formed from this language have survived in modern Wiltshire. For simplicity all of these names are described with the one word, Welsh. Of 27 significant river and stream names in the county, 19 are of this type. Examples include the **Avon** (from abona or river) and the **Nadder** (from notr, or flowing).

Wiltshire is on the border area between the east of England, where such names are less frequent and the south-west, where they form a more significant proportion of place-names. Of all the surviving Welsh river names in England, 4.3% are in Wiltshire. This compares with 2% in Hampshire and 1.3% in Berkshire, but 5% in Dorset and 6.4% in Somerset.

As well as names for rivers, Welsh place-names survive for other natural features such as hills (eg the old name for **Clarendon Forest** until the 15th century was **Penchet**, from the Primitive Welsh pennged, meaning end of the wood). Fewer survive in the actual names of settlements.

Despite almost 400 years of Roman rule, few Latin place-names survive. The only modern place-name which has developed from one we know was used by the Romans is **Salisbury**. Here the Roman name of **Sorvio-dunum** developed into the Saxon **Searoburg**, becoming **Sarisberie** in 1086 (Domesday Book). The later change of the 'r' to 'l' took place through the influence of Norman-French.

However, it is possible that some other words of Latin were understood by the Anglo-Saxons, who heard them being used. The place-names **Fovant**, **Teffont** and **Urchfont** (as well as **Fonthill**, west of Teffont) come from the Latin fontana which was probably used to describe a well, or water channel. In addition, **Wickham Green** may contain the Latin vicus. This particular type of name may have been used to describe an

Anglo-Saxon settlement near a surviving Roman one. When Latin appears in other place-names, such as the second part of **Teffont Magna** (from the Latin for large, important) it dates from the later Middle Ages.

Like the Romans, the Norman conquerors created few place-names but changed and altered many which had existed before them. **Devizes** is one of the few names in England to be created from Norman-French. It is from the French devises, meaning boundary. Most other French elements in place-names date from after the Norman Conquest, when the names of French-speaking landowners were added to existing Saxon place-names. Examples include **Winterbourne Dauntsey** (named after Roger Daunteseye, 1242) and **Sutton Mandeville** (after Robert de Mandevill, in 1236)

Most place-names can be placed into one of a number of different types.

1. Topographical names: these describe the location of the place. In the Saxon period, for example, there were over 36 different words used to describe types of hills, ridges and slopes. (The most common hill words are dun, heafod, ofer; eg **Baydon, Donhead**.) Other place-names describe water sources, valleys, roads and tracks, woods and clearings, ploughland and pasture.

2. Habitative names: these describe the kind of settlement itself. An example is ham, from which the modern word home comes and originally meaning farm and later village (eg **Corsham**). It is a fairly rare word in Wiltshire. The word tun is the most common word of this type (eg **Dinton**). Like ham its meaning changed over time. Other habitative words include cot, (cottage, or shelter), worth, (homestead/hamlet) and stoc (probably meaning dependent settlement, or cattle/dairy farm).

3. Ownership place-names, which indicate the name of the owner of the estate. Many of these probably date from the 10th century onwards and are not the names of the leaders of the first pioneering settlers in an area. There is growing evidence which suggests that in the 9th and 10th centuries there was an expansion of rural settlement, probably associated with the breaking-in of new arable land, the establishment of open-field farming, the division of larger estates and the increasing number of small noblemen, or thegns (see **Fiddington, Fifield, Fyfield, Tinhead**). It is likely that a large number of the tun names, when linked to a personal name, represent this new kind of settlement pattern and that those place-

names formed from worth, cot and the rarer hiwisc (eg **Huish**, **Hardenhuish**) represent the earlier, smaller and more scattered settlements.

It is the landowners that are recorded in these place-names, not the poorer and more numerous class of peasant farmers. Some of these personal names (especially the short forms of other, longer, names) are not recorded outside of place-names. Some may not be personal names at all, but corruptions of other words. The issue is still open to debate.

Place-names open windows on the past. The name of **Wansdyke** for example records the name of the Anglo-Saxon god Woden and is a survival from pagan times. Other evidence indicates the cultural mix in early England. **Walcot**, near Swindon, means the cottage of the Welsh; in AD 961 a road in **Burbage** was named **Wealeweg** (the 'Welsh road') and Avebury was described as **Waledich** (the 'Welsh ditch') as late as 1289.

We can use place-names to discover information about what crops were grown, what animals were kept, the extent of woodland, the conversion of pasture land to arable farming, who owned the land, what the land looked like – all in the distant past. Place-names are a historic treasure chest waiting to be carefully unlocked. This guide gives an opportunity to begin that fascinating and enjoyable process.

Martyn J. Whittock

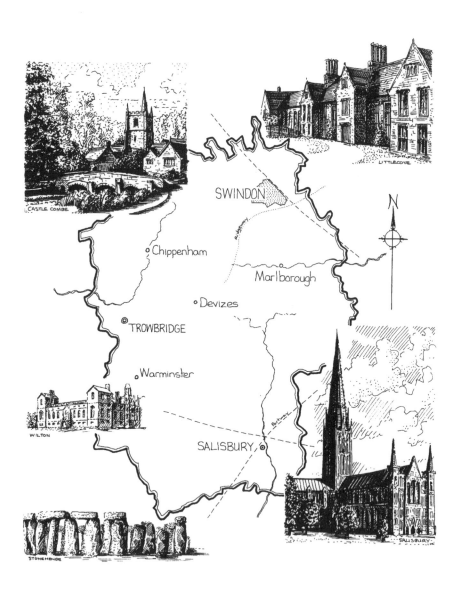

CASTLE COMBE

LITTLECOTE

SWINDON

Chippenham

Marlborough

Devizes

TROWBRIDGE

Warminster

WILTON

SALISBURY

SALISBURY

STONEHENGE

N

·· A ··

❧ ALDBOURNE

First recorded as Ealdincburnan, in 970, the name is Saxon and means the burna (stream) of Ealda. By the time of the Domesday Book (1086) the name had developed into Aldeborne, though later spellings include Audiburne (1217) and Audingeburn (1226). This last spelling (using the plural 'inge', as opposed to the singular 'ing') may show the name, now pronounced 'Auburn', refers to Ealda's people. The village is famous for its church, as St Michael's has the largest Norman doorway of any parish church in Wiltshire.

South Street in the village has had this name since at least 1553 and **West Street** since 1614. A 16th century manor house at Upper Upham may stand on the site of an earlier building which was associated with the 14th century John of Gaunt.

The village was famous for its bell foundry which between 1642 and 1826 made bells for many churches in Wiltshire and in surrounding counties. Rural crafts such as straw and willow plaiting survived here until the 20th century.

Aldbourne Four Barrows is a group of three bell barrows and a bowl barrow. One of the barrows contained a cremated adult and the bones of a pig; the others a cremated adult and a bone pin; two skeletons, a grooved dagger and a tanged arrow head; and another adult cremation together with a small pot, amber beads and a bone pin. Two other barrows produced a fine incense cup – now known as the Aldbourne cup – and other finds including fragments of a bronze dagger.

Nearby **Snap** is first recorded in 1268 as Snape and is derived from a Saxon word snaep (boggy land). **Sugar Hill** is far from being a sweet name as the 1591 spelling – Shuger waie – reveals. It comes from the Saxon word sceacere and meant path of the robbers (later hill of the robbers). **Peaks Wood** probably describes a wood which had a very angular shape. It was Pikewode in 1289. **Upham** is first recorded in 955 as Uphammere. It probably means something like the high boundary, containing the Saxon word 'gemaere' (boundary). **The Dean** was originally

Sheephouse dean in 1650 and contains the Saxon word 'denu' (large valley), while **Giants Grave** refers to a large burial mound.

✾ ALDERBURY

This means Aethelwaru's burg (fort). The name is Saxon and the personal name is that of a woman. Saxon women could be important landowners. It first appeared in 972, when it was called Aethelwarebyrig. By 1341 its appearance had become Alrebury and by 1531 a more familiar Aldersbury. The **Green Dragon** pub was used by Charles Dickens as the model for the Blue Dragon in *Martin Chuzzlewit* (1843). Local legend claims that **The Three Crowns** takes its title from an event in 1357 when King Edward III entertained the captured kings of France and Scotland in nearby Clarendon Palace. However, it probably takes its name from the Biblical Wise Men who visited the baby Jesus.

Ivy Church was first recorded in the Latin form Monasterium Hedorosum in 1109, though by 1327 it appeared in Middle English as Ivychirche. Clearly the growth of ivy on the building must have been very striking. **Treasurer's Dean** belonged to the Treasurer of Salisbury Cathedral. It is first recorded in 1650 as Treasurer's Copps.

✾ ALDERTON

This means the 'tun' (settlement) of Ealdhere, a Saxon. It was first recorded in the Domesday Book in the form Aldri(n)tone.

Cranehill Wood actually takes its name from crows not cranes. The 1317 spelling – Crawenhulle – shows it ultimately derives from a Saxon word 'crawena' (crows). **Hugh's Farm** is named from the 18th century Hughes family. **Townfield Farm**, at the end of the village, is first recorded in 1840 as Town Field and means the field belonging to the township (ie the village).

✾ ALLINGTON

There are three places in Wiltshire with this name. They all have different meanings! This shows up in their early spellings, and demonstrates how problematic it is to attempt the analysis of place-name origins on the basis of modern spellings alone. It is always necessary to examine early spellings. Even then it is helpful to look at a number of examples as some early spellings may be corrupt. This is especially true of some Domesday Book spellings, since Saxon words sounded alien to Norman-French scribes, resulting in the recording of misleading versions of some place-names. All this shows how challenging place-name study can be at times!

One **Allington** is north-east of Devizes. It first appears in Domesday Book as Adelington. It is from the Saxon words aetheling (prince) and tun (settlement). It obviously belonged to one of the ruling families of Anglo-Saxon England. The unusually named **The Gog** in the parish is near a stream and means boggy ground. **Child's Farm** takes its name from a 17th century family-name, Childe.

Another, called Alentone in the Domesday Book, is south-east of Amesbury. It may mean the tun (settlement) of Ealda, probably a Saxon landowner. However, this name may be from the Saxon word ealdan (old) and mean 'the old settlement'. It is hard to be sure. Nearby **Wyndham's Farm** takes its name from a local farming family.

The last place is situated north-west of Chippenham. Like the rest it contains the Saxon word tun (settlement). This one is named after a Saxon lord named Aella. In the Domesday Book it is spelled Allentone.

❧ ALTON (BARNES and PRIORS)

First recorded, as Aweltun, in 825, the name means the settlement at the source of a river. It is from two Saxon words 'awiell' and 'tun'.

Alton Barnes takes its name from the Berners family, who were Norman landowners here. The name of **Alton Priors** reminds us that the land here was once owned by the priory of St Swithun, Winchester. **Adam's Grave** is the name of a prehistoric long barrow and is a Christianised name, the former being Woden's barrow (Saxon Wodnesbeorge), named after the pagan Saxon god. When the barrow was opened in 1860 parts of possibly four skeletons were found along with a leaf-shaped arrow-head.

Red Shore takes its name from the Saxon word 'sceard' (gap) and refers to where the Ridgeway passes through the Wansdyke. An Anglo-Saxon charter shows that it was sometimes also called readgeat, which has the same meaning. The word 'red' refers to the soil colour. **Workway Drove** derives from a Saxon original, geweorc weg and means the road by the fortress. It refers to the hillfort on **Knap Hill**. On top of this hill lies the first causewayed camp ever recognised in Britain. These camps date from the New Stone Age and were seasonal communal meeting places. At Knap Hill a date of 3500 BC was produced by carbon dating some of the fragments of bone found in the ditches.

The **Wandsdyke** runs through Alton Priors parish and its name means the dic (dyke) of the pagan Saxon god Woden. The name of this god was also linked to two other places in the parish. We have already noted Adam's Grave and a gap in the Wansdyke was called Woddesgeat (Woden's gate). In nearby West Overton parish what is now Hursley Bottom was once called Wodnesdene (Woden's large valley). Why the god's name was so associated with this area is a mystery.

❧ ALVEDISTON

When this was first recorded in 1167 it was spelled Alfwieteston. It means Aelfgeat's tun (settlement). Aelfgeat is a Saxon name. It was Alvideston in 1190 though later versions of the name included the abbreviated forms Alston (1571) and Awston (1585)

Norrington means the northern settlement, from a Saxon name northantun. **Trow Farm** probably means at the trough, referring to a landscape feature, derived from a Saxon word trogan. Later it seems to have been confused with a Saxon word treow (trees).

❧ AMESBURY

This was first written as Ambresbyrig in 880 and there is no agreement about what the name means. The second part is easy – it is the Saxon word burg (fort). The first part is more difficult. It might be a man's name (Ambre), or the Saxon word for a bird – the yellow hammer. Some writers think it commemorates the name of a Dark Age Welsh hero, Ambrosius. Welsh legends claim this, as did the medieval writer Geoffrey of Monmouth. Other legends claim that, after the death of King Arthur, his

Stonehenge

wife, Guinevere, retired to a monastery here. Lancelot visited her but she was so sorry she had betrayed her husband she refused to kiss him and they never met again. **Countess Road**, now the A345, has been called this since the 14th century. It was named after Alice de Lacy, Countess of Lincoln, who owned the land at Amesbury. The town was once famous for its manufacture of clay tobacco pipes.

Cursus Barrows are so named because they stand near a parallel earth bank (the Cursus) which runs towards Stonehenge. Excavations here found burials accompanied by weapons and beads. The graves date from the Bronze Age. **Old and New King Barrows** probably take their name from an otherwise lost legend associated with these burial mounds.

Together they amount to seven Bronze Age barrows. **Ratfyn** has nothing to do with rodents but takes its name from a Saxon original meaning Hrotha's marsh. The strange field-name **Tumbling Bay**, first recorded in 1676, probably refers to the movement of water associated with the nearby river Avon.

Stonehenge means either stone hinge, referring to the great trilithons where two upright stones support a third stone, or stone gallows, from the Saxon word hen(c)gen. This last meaning is probably most likely. This is perhaps the most famous prehistoric archaeological site in Britain. It was built in stages from 2800 BC until 1500 BC. Its purpose remains obscure. The presence of many axe carvings may suggest that some form of symbolic axe worship formed part of the rituals practised here. It was aligned on the midsummer sunrise and the midwinter sunset and this may suggest more about the key points in the pagan ritual year here. In the popular imagination the site is associated with the Iron Age Druids but in fact use of the site predates the Druids by almost 2,000 years. By their day it was almost certainly in ruins.

Vespasian's Camp is a name for a nearby hillfort. It takes its name from the Roman general who campaigned in the West Country in the 1st century AD. However this is not an ancient name but rather an antiquarian invention.

🌑 ANSTY

This unusual name first appeared as Anestige, in the Domesday Book. It is from a Saxon word 'anstiga', used to describe a stretch of road on which other roads converged. By 1245 it was spelled Ansteia. There is a legend that a blind fiddler entered a mysterious passage at Ansty which led underground and from which he never emerged. According to the legend the music of his playing could be heard long after he vanished.

Waterloo Barn was Cholen Barn in 1773 but later took on the name of the famous victory of Wellington over Napoleon in 1815.

Coombe contains the Saxon word 'cumb', which refers to a short, broad valley. Such valleys were usually shorter and broader than those described by the Saxon word 'denu'. Valleys called cumb were usually rather out of the way.

ASHTON

There are a number of places meaning the ashtree settlement: **Ashton Gifford**, **Ashton Keynes**, **Steeple Ashton**, **Rood Ashton** and **West Ashton**. They all contain the common word tun (settlement) and the Saxon word aesc (ash tree). Because they were common names some had another word added in the Middle Ages to tell them apart.

Ashton Gifford is from Elias Giffard, the owner of the village in 1242. **Wraxworthy Barn** takes its name from a local family-name, Raxworthy. **Ashton Keynes** is from Henry Kaignel, who owned the village in 1242. **Kent End** does not take its name from the county but from Ralph Kent, a 14th century landowner. **Ashton Down** was just plain 'the Down' in the 16th century, and **Ashtonfield** was once broken up into Eastfield and Westfield, the large open fields before enclosure.

Steeple Ashton reminds us of the magnificent 15th century village church. **Drove Lane** in the village dates from at least the 14th century when it was le Drove. By 1526 it had become le Drovelane, a road along which cattle were driven. **Mudmead Lane** takes its name from a nearby field, called Mudmede furlong in 1491. **Amouracre** probably means field of the yellow hammer from the Saxon word 'amore', the name of the bird. **Spiers Piece** takes its name from the Spire family who lived here in the early 17th century. **Abury** has had its name contracted since 1262 when it was Aldebury in Stepulashton. It is Saxon and means the old fort.

West Ashton parish contains a number of interesting names. **Rood Ashton** – now famous for Rood Ashton House – refers to a stone cross, from the Saxon word 'rodestan'. It is first mentioned by this name in an Anglo-Saxon charter. **Kettle Lane Cottages** actually derive from 'spring of the kids'. The name also survives in the nearby field-name of **Kittles**. **Yarnbrook** now stands on the busy Trowbridge to Westbury road and means beyond the brook. In the 14th century it was Yondebrok. In Wiltshire the Saxon word 'broc' (brook) is used of darker streams flowing through the claylands, the word 'burna' being reserved for the clear streams of the chalk country. **Flowers Wood** is from a 15th century family name, Flowre. **Crosswelldown Farm** actually contains the word crow and in 1663 it was Crowswell Down. **The Drove** was originally Motweye in the 13th century when it led to the moot – the meeting place of the local area. **Stourton Plantation** reveals that the former owners of Stourhead once owned land here.

❋ ATWORTH

First recorded in 1001 as Attenwrthe, it means Aetta's homestead, from the name of a Saxon – Aetta – and the Saxon word worth. In 1451 it was called Mechell (large) Attewarde and in 1458 Great Atte Ward. However, this name did not survive. The small museum, in the dovecote at Poplar Farm, contains evidence from the village's past, ranging from a Roman villa to local quarrying.

Great and **Little Chalfield** mean the cold open land, from a Saxon original cealdfeld.

Cottles House was once a separate manor named Attelworth Parva in 1298 (little Atworth) to differentiate it from the main settlement. By 1402 it had become Atteworth Cotell after a local landowner and by 1412 the simpler name Cotelys first made an appearance. It was a version of this shorter name that stuck.

Linch Bottom takes its name from the Saxon word hlinc (a terrace, or ridge). **The Hayes** is first recorded in 1573 as le Heyes and probably comes from the Saxon word gehaeg (enclosure), while **Lenton Farm** probably means the flax farm.

❋ AVEBURY

First spelled as Avreberie in the Domesday Book, it is Saxon and means Affa's burg (fort). It is famous for the huge bank and ditch surrounding the prehistoric stone circles here. This is one of the most striking archaeological sites in Europe and the internal ditch originally measured some 9m in depth and 21m wide at the top! Inside the earth bank, or henge, are the remains of three stone circles, including the largest in Britain. Avebury was in use from about 2600 BC to 1600 BC. In the Middle Ages many of the stones were destroyed or buried. When excavated one revealed the crushed body of a man killed when it fell on him in the 14th century. It seems that the stones were regarded as threatening because of the pagan rituals once practised at the site. Later, in the 17th century, there were more efforts to remove the stones.

The first Saxon settlers must have thought that it was a fort. In 1289 it was called Waledich, meaning the Welsh ditch. This is because before Wiltshire was settled by the Saxons it was inhabited by British people, whom the Saxons called the Welsh.

Many local finds are now housed in the Alexander Keiller Museum which contains artifacts discovered by Alexander Keiller at Avebury, Windmill Hill and West Kennet Avenue when he excavated between 1924 and 1929 and again between 1934 and 1939. At the nearby Great Barn Museum the Wiltshire Folk Life Society's collection is displayed within a barn which dates from about 1690. There are displays of thatching, blacksmithing, saddlery and dairying amongst many other fascinating reminders of Wiltshire rural life.

Avebury Manor is reputed to be built on the site of a Benedictine cell. The present house dates from the late 1550s and was extended in the 17th century. It is set in gardens containing topiary, fine borders, a wishing well and fountains. Charles II and later Queen Anne stayed here. Many of the rooms are panelled in oak and some contain noteworthy plaster ceilings. In the house are portraits of Wiltshire gentlemen, the bed reputed to have been slept in by Queen Anne and a travelling chest which once belonged to Mary Tudor. There is now a museum here.

Nearby **Silbury Hill** takes its name either from the Saxon word burg (fort) or beorg (burial mound). The first part of the name is obscure and the name is not known before the 13th century. It is the largest prehistoric mound in the country. Why it was built and what it was used for remain mysteries. Excavations have failed to find any trace of a burial. A local legend claims it was built with unbelievable speed, while a pot of milk was boiling! Another legend claims it was made by the devil on his way to dump the soil on Devizes. Other myths claim that a man in golden armour is buried inside the hill.

Beckhampton was Bachentune in the Domesday Book. It is a Saxon name and probably refers to a stream flowing to the Kennet. It would then mean something like village of the people by the stream.

West Kennett was Chenete in the Domesday Book and takes its name from the nearby river. It became Westkenete by 1288. The New Stone Age long barrow here is 100m long and 2.5m high. Excavations in 1955-56 discovered a large number of burials. Strikingly it was clear that the bones had been stripped of flesh before being placed here and many were carefully sorted so that similar bones were grouped together in different chambers of the tomb. Altogether the tomb may have been in use for about 1,000 years.

Waden Hill probably derives from Saxon weohdun (hill with a heathen temple). Given its close proximity to the prehistoric site at Avebury the name is not surprising.

·· B ··

❊ BADBURY

King Arthur may be linked to this village! The name is from the Saxon Badda's burg (fort). The village name was clearly once the name of the hillfort, now called Liddington Castle. Possibly it is a Saxon version of a place – Mount Badon – mentioned by the Dark Age writer Gildas as the site of a great British victory over the Anglo-Saxons. Later writers thought Arthur was commander of the British at this battle. There are five other Badburys in England, from Lincolnshire to Dorset. Who Badda was is completely unknown.

Nearby **Baydon** – possibly from the Saxon begdun (berryhill) – may alternatively be related to the name of the mysterious battle of Mount Badon. The matter is undecided.

❊ BARFORD ST MARTIN

Recorded in Domesday Book as Bereford the name is from the Saxon for barley ford. It was Berevord St Martin in 1304.

Hurdcott is the cot (cottage) of the herdsmen and is Saxon. It is first recorded in Domesday Book as Hardicote.

❊ BAVERSTOCK

While there may seem a passing resemblance to 'beaver' in this name, the 968 spelling Babbanstoc shows it to derive from Babba's stoc (outlying farm). The same name appears in the place-name Bapton.

❧ BEDWYN, GREAT and LITTLE

This simply means Bindweed – the place where bindweed grows! The Wiltshire dialect word for this weed is 'bedwind'. In 778 the name was recorded as Bedewinde and by 1437 it had become Bedewyn.

At Great Bedwyn **Brail Farm** is derived from a medieval word for a wood stocked with deer. **Hatchet Lane** takes its name from the Saxon word haecc (gate leading into a wood). **Stoke House** derives from the Saxon word stocc (stump).

At Little Bedwyn **Chisbury** means either the cis (gravel) burg (fort), or the fort belonging to Cissa. All the elements are Saxon. **Puthall Farm** is also Saxon, meaning the halh (hollow) of Putta. **Little Frith** takes its name from the Saxon word fyrhthe (woodland) and the form Fithwode (Frithwood) recorded in 1257 supports this.

❧ BEMERTON

An unusual name, this is derived from the Saxon bymeretun (trumpeter's settlement). The same first word is also found in the lost name Bymeracumb, in Downton. Both were probably land given to the servants who led the king's hunt. In the Domesday Book it was spelled Bimertone and later Beomertona (1107), Bimbertone (1259) and Bimmerton (1553).

Another unusual name is that of **Fugglestone**, derived from the Saxon tun (settlement) of the fugol (bird). This may have been a personal name.

Quidhampton is also Saxon and means the haematun (settlement of the people) where cwead (dung) is found. It must have been a farm famous for its manure. The second element may be hamtun (home-farm).

❧ BERWICK (BASSETT, ST JAMES, ST JOHN and ST LEONARD)

A popular Saxon name, it is derived from berewic (barley farm). Berewic was used to describe an oulying part of an estate. It is found four times in Wiltshire. In three cases the church dedication is used to tell the settlements apart.

Berwick Bassett. This settlement takes its name from Alan Basset, who owned the land here in 1211. In the graveyard sarsen stones have been used as tombstones. The church of St Nicholas has a low two stage tower and is recognisable by its blunt pyramid top. Inside there is a 13th century font, a 15th century screen that has been restored and a later clerk's reading desk.

Berwick St James. First recorded as Berewyke Sancti Jacobi in 1190. Nearby **Asserton** is Saxon and means Aeschere's tun (settlement).

Berwick St John was Berwicha in 1167 and was first called Berewyke S. Johannis in 1265. Nearby **Bridmore** takes its name from the Saxon Bryda's mere (lake, or pond). The same landowner also gave his name to Brydinga dic (ditch) mentioned in a charter dated 955. **Easton Farm** is the east tun (settlement). **Rushmore** is the rush mere, and **Tinkley Down** the leah (clearing) of Tilluc, while **Winklebury Camp** is the burg (fort) used in winter, a meaning clear in the 955 spelling, Winterburge. This is an unfinished promontory fort dating from the Iron Age. It seems to have been constructed in three phases; in the final phase it was reduced in size to about 1.8ha and given two entrances. **Chettles Clift** takes its name from the Saxon word for kettle, describing a landscape feature. **Frying Pan** was Frying Pan Coppice in 1840 and probably describes the shape of a wood. **Rotherley Down** is from the Saxon words hryther (cattle) and leah (clearing). **Uddens Coppice** was Iweden in 1227 and is the Yew denu (large valley).

Berwick St Leonard was once called Cold Berwick and this appears in 1545 in the form Cold Barwyke. The name survives in **Cold Berwick Hill**. The form with the church dedication first appears in 1291.

✤ BIDDESTONE

Named after a Saxon landowner, the village name means Biedin's tun (settlement). It was spelled Bedestone in the Domesday Book. Later spellings show an interesting variety of forms including Biedestone (1297), Butteston (1428), Bittson (1539). The church of St Nicholas has interesting late Georgian woodwork. The nave, chancel and sanctuary descend in steps and the 13th century bell turret base has a 15th century spirelet.

Weavern Farm contains the name of the man who owned the land here in 1332, William de Wevere. **The Butts** may be a reference to medieval archery. **Erkwell Wood** probably is a corruption from a Saxon original meaning spring of the hare.

❧ BISHOPSTONE (near SWINDON)

Bissopeston in 1186, this means the tun (settlement) belonging to the Bishop of Ramsbury

Starveall Farm is a fairly common name and refers to a farm with disappointing productivity.

❧ BISHOPSTONE (near SALISBURY)

Identical meaning; in 1166 it was Bissopeston.

Croucheston may be a combination of two words, a Welsh word cruc (hill) and a Saxon word tun (settlement).

Faulston was Fallerstone in 1275 and is a combination of a French personal name, Fallard, and the Saxon word tun (settlement). This shows how the word 'tun' was used in the creation of place-names both before and after the Norman Conquest of 1066.

Flamston Farm. The same is true of this name as it links the personal name of William Flambard, who owned land here in 1202, with the word tun (settlement). **Throop Farm** takes its name from the Saxon word thorp. In the Saxon period this had the meaning of farm. A related word with a similar meaning was also used by Viking settlers, and is common in place-names in the Midlands and north.

Barrow House takes its name from a location called Barwe in 1224 and derived from the Saxon word beorg (hill, burial mound).

❧ BLUNSDON (ST ANDREW and BROAD BLUNSDON)

Both names mean Blunt's dun (hill) and are Saxon in origin. The name St Andrew refers to the church dedication, while Broad means the chief of the two settlements. The name first appears in the Domesday Book in the form Bluntesdone. During its history Broad Blunsdon briefly had the alternative names Hangingebluntesdon (1242) and Blountesdon Gay (1348). Blunsdon St Andrew was called Churibluntesdon (referring to 'church') in 1242 but appeared as Bluntesdon Seynt Andreu in 1281, an alternative name which replaced the former. According to local legend it is from Blunsdon that Oliver Cromwell reputedly used artillery in an attempt to hit the church at Highworth. There is no factual basis for this legend. Traditionally Cromwell is often blamed for the destruction of churches, for which he actually was not responsible. Such legends are probably products of the fact that Puritans were antagonistic to the established church, combined with a confusion of Oliver Cromwell with Thomas Cromwell, Henry VIII's minister who was responsible for the dissolution of the monasteries.

Groundwell House takes its name from the Grundwylle (Saxon for deep spring), first recorded in 962.

Burytown Farm refers to the 'burg' (fort) on nearby **Castle Hill**. **Fowler's Farm** is named after a 13th century landholder here. **Newland's Farm** has been 'new' since the time of King Henry IV, around 1400! **St Leonard's Farm** takes its name from the chapel of St Leonard in Broad Blunsdon. The chapel is first mentioned in 1291.

❧ BOSCOMBE

Possibly short, broad valley where burrs grow, from the Saxon words bors and cumb. The first word possibly may be the Saxon word box (box-tree). The word cumb may be linked to the Saxon word for cup, or related to a Welsh word cwm (small bowl-like hollow). It is frequently used in Wiltshire for short, broad, fairly shallow valleys. In the Domesday Book it was called Boscumbe. The famous Church of England theologian, Richard Hooker, was rector here in the 16th century and part of his house survives in the present vicarage.

✿ BOX

The first spelling of this name – Bocza, in 1144 – conceals the fact that it just means the box-tree, from a Saxon word for the tree. By 1181 a more familiar spelling – la Boxe – appeared, though in 1216 a less familiar form la Bosse was used, but did not survive. It is now famous for the Box Tunnel, built by Brunel and carrying the railway line to London. **Hatt House Barrows** are supposed to be the graves of three kings. When archaeological excavations took place on nearby Totney Hill in the 1930s the archaeologists were told by one old local that they would find nothing there because the three kings were buried at Hatt House. There are a number of such traditions associated with prehistoric barrows in Wiltshire. These legends may arise from two sources: one is an attempt to explain barrows by making them the graves of a social elite, which makes a lot of sense; the other is a folk memory of a time when England was indeed divided into smaller units, each having its own ruler.

Chapel Plaister was first mentioned in 1268 and its name is derived from the Saxon plegstede (a place to play). This may have referred to a village green used for communal games. The first half of the name points to the fact that there was once a chapel here belonging to Glastonbury Abbey.

Ditteridge is from a Saxon original, dichrycg (ditch ridge) and is probably a landscape description. **Hazelbury House** is an old name and the site was called Heselberi in 1001. It is the hazel fort from a Saxon original 'burg'.

Henley means the high leah (clearing) and has carried this name since at least the 13th century. The fact that leah is a Saxon word may indicate that the name is a lot older, or may simply indicate a continued medieval use of this common name-forming element.

Rudloe is the ridgehill and is Saxon. It is now the site of RAF Rudloe Manor. **Slade's Farm** does not, as it appears, take its name from a former farmer but from the Saxon word slaed (short valley). **Wadswick** indicates that it was the wic (dairy farm) of an otherwise unknown Saxon landowner. **Wormwood Farm** is a Saxon name and means the geard (enclosure) of the snake, or dragon. This use of the Saxon word 'wyrm' may refer to an otherwise unknown legend concerning the area.

Of the nearby woodland **Charlwood** means wood of the ceorls (lowest class of peasant cultivators in the Saxon period). **Ennox Wood** refers to land broken in from wild countryside.

✹ BOYTON

Recorded in Domesday Book as Boientone, the name is Saxon and means Boia's tun (settlement). A more recognisable spelling appears in 1366 – Boynton. The church of St Mary has a great wheel window in the Gifford Chapel. The style of this feature is called early geometric – with circles within circles – and dates from around 1280. There is also fine 14th century tracery elsewhere in the church.

Corton is the tun (settlement) of Cort. **Manor Farm** was called East Corton in 1356, while **West Farm** was named West Corton in 1281. **Boyton Bridge** has carried this name since at least 1514. **Chattle Hole** actually means kettle hole and describes a landscape feature. **Starveall** is a fairly common field-name and refers to poor ground.

✹ BRADFORD ON AVON

This lovely wool-town, with its honey coloured houses, terraced above the river Avon, was the site of the battle of Bradanforda be Afne, in 652. A Saxon name, it means the broad ford on the river Avon. It contains a fine Anglo-Saxon church, dating from around 1000. The curiously named area of **Tory** takes its name from the same Celtic word that describes high places in the west of England (eg Glastonbury Tor, the tors of Dartmoor). **Budbury** overlooking the Avon is derived from the Saxon name Budda's burg (fort). In the Domesday Book it was spelled Bodeberie. **Wooley Street** is from an area where wolves were found in the leah (clearing), though in 1426 it was called Seynt Olesstret. **Market Street** has been called by this name since at least 1612; **High Street** since 1660. **St Margaret Street** takes its name from the medieval Hospital of St Margaret. The town bridge is first recorded in 1426 as Avenbrygge. The river-name **Avon** is Welsh and found twice in Wiltshire. The modern Welsh version of the name is Afon and its roots lie in the name Abona, meaning quite simply 'river'.

An interesting example of how old field-names can be taken as the street-names of modern housing developments is found on Southway Park, a small housing estate on the south side of the town. Here names such as

Bradford-on-Avon

Bassetts Pasture, **Barn Piece**, **Piplar Ground** and **Folly Field** refer to local field names. That of Folly Field refers to a name which also occurs in the form **The Folly**, describing an area of land on the Trowbridge Road, and shown on the first edition of the Ordnance Survey, 1817.

Cumberwell, now the site of a golf course, was first recorded in the Domesday Book as Cubrewell and is Saxon, meaning the wiell (spring) of the Welshman. The Saxon word Cumbra (Welsh) was an alternative to the more usual term Walh/Wealh, especially as that term had come in time to mean a slave.

Elms Cross on the outskirts of Bradford, on the Frome Road, is first recorded in 1630 as Elmes Cros. The second word may refer to a crossing of ways or to a croft.

Widbrook, now the site of a marina and the strikingly named **Gongoozler** pub and restaurant, means Wicga's broc (brook). The Saxon word broc was used of the darker streams flowing through the claylands, as opposed to burna which in Wiltshire is used of the clearer streams of the chalk country.

❄ BRADLEY, MAIDEN

This Saxon name was originally brad (wide) leah (clearing). The earliest use of leah was for woodland but it usually meant clearing, or glade and later could be used for pasture, or meadow. Here it apparently was used for a clearing. The word Maiden probably refers to a monastic hospital for women, mentioned there in 1227. The lepresses of Bradley were given the right to collect wood in Selwood Forest in 1232. The name was Bradelie in the Domesday Book, Braddeley in 1316 and Maydenbradley in 1547.

Church Street was spelled Chyrche strete in 1509. **Honeypot Lane** was a nickname for a sticky trackway but made so by mud not bees!

Kate's Bench Clump has nothing to do with a woman's name as the spelling of 1385 – Cattenbenche – shows. It actually means wildcat slope/hill. **Yarnfield** may mean open country where eagles are found, from a Saxon name earnafeld, or perhaps takes its name from a river-name such as Gerne.

❄ BRADLEY, NORTH

This has the same meaning as above. Nearby **Brokerswood** – now a woodland activity centre – takes its name from the Saxon words brocc (badger) and yfer (bank).

Ireland is probably so called because it is a distant part of the parish. It has been known as this since at least 1802. Nearby, in Southwick parish, the neighbouring farm is called **Scotland**.

Cutteridge means the hrycg (ridge) of Cuda and appeared in 1241 in the spelling Cuderuge.

Honeybridge Farm is a name dating from at least the 13th century. It may either refer to bees or to sticky soil; it is difficult to tell which is the more likely. Alternatively it may derive from a Saxon personal name, Huna.

❋ BRATTON

Settlement by newly cultivated land, from Saxon braectun. The name was spelled Bratton in 1177 but later went through a number of variations including Bracton (1196), Brotton (1227) and Bretton (1241) before arriving back at the original spelling. The church of St James has a varied selection of carvings which date from the 15th century. Behind the village is the striking figure of a white horse cut into the chalk of the rising scarp of Salisbury Plain and usually termed the 'Westbury White Horse'. A revel used to be held to accompany the scouring of the horse to keep it visible. There is controversy as to how old this particular horse is; local legend claims it to be carved by the people of Alfred the Great to celebrate his victory over the Vikings at nearby Edington. But there is documentary evidence to suggest it was either cut, or recut, in the 18th century to give the rather realistic horse that we now see. This is significant as the present horse has nothing of the dynamic movement and stylistic lines of Uffington White Horse in Oxfordshire. So, it may be that the horse is no more than an 18th century work and the Bratton revel established in imitation of the very old and very famous 'Scouring of the White Horse' held at Uffington. Only detailed excavation at the site would decide whether the current horse is the original, or has replaced a more ancient carving.

Despite local legends **Danes Lye** has nothing to do with the Vikings defeated by Alfred the Great at nearby Edington. Instead it is derived from two Saxon words denu (large valley) and leah (clearing).
Dunge as its name suggests is a reference to farmyard manure. In 1395 it was called Dengestret.

Melbourne House is named after a stream called the Mill Stream. Another stream in the vicinity was called the Ewelm, meaning the source. **Patcombe Hill** takes its name from a boundary marker recorded in 968 as padecan stan, Padeca's stone. **Redlands Farm** does not refer to the colour red but to reeds. The orginal would have been the Saxon word hreod (reed).

❋ BREMHILL

This is from the Saxon word bremel (bramble). Despite the appearance of the name there is no reference to hill in the original record of the name. This was in 937 and the place was called just plain Broemel. However, by 1430 the name had been changed to Bremhill and, despite a spelling in 1637 that was a throwback to the real meaning (Bremble), it was Bremhill that stuck. Nearby **Bremhill Wick** would have been a wic (dairy farm) associated with the village.

Avon takes its name from the river. **Cadenham** means the ham (settlement) of Cada and is one of the rare uses of the Saxon word ham in Wiltshire. The more usual word found in the place-names of the county is tun.

Charlcote is first recorded in 1300 as Cherlecote and means the cot (cottage) of the free peasants. The Saxon word ceorl described the lowest grade of peasant freemen. **Ennix Wood** refers to land brought into cultivation or use and is found in a number of minor place-names in Wiltshire.

Foxham means, much as its name suggests, either the ham (village) or hamm (land in the bend of a river) of the foxes. It is situated on a small tributary of the river Avon so hamm is more likely, especially given the relative rarity of the use of the word ham in Wiltshire.

Godsell Farm probably means God's Hill, though why the name should have been chosen is unknown. Alternatively a Saxon name Godus may be relevant here. **Hare Street Farm** takes its name from a Saxon original, herestraet (army-road). The unusual name **Honeybed Wood**, once Honybett Coppice in 1564, is probably a reference to soft ground.

Spirthill probably refers to a spring. The earliest spelling – Speerful in 1065 – is less useful in deciding its origins than later spellings, such as that from 1153, Spertella.

Stanley is derived from a Saxon name stanleah (stony clearing). **Stanley Bridge** is first recorded with that name in 1570. Earlier (in 1348) it had been Stanleyesforde.

Stockham Marsh derives from the Saxon words stocc (stump) and hamm (land in the bend of a river). It was plain Stokham in 1289 but appears as Stokeham marshe in 1553.

❧ BRITFORD

This is probably derived from the Saxon words bryda (bride) and ford. Situated on the river Avon, south-east of Salisbury, it might refer to a routeway used to a church for weddings. There is a faint possibility that it may contain the Saxon word Bryttan. It would then mean ford of the British. This would refer to people living in the area when the first Anglo-Saxon settlers arrived. When the church of St Peter was restored in 1873 three Anglo-Saxon doorways were revealed, one of which had re-used Roman tiles. In addition the church has an altar tomb which is reputedly that of Henry Stafford who was beheaded in 1483.

Longford Castle was plain Langeford when the Domesday Book was compiled and takes its name from the length of the ford across a wide stretch of the Avon.

There is a West Indian connection with **Kitts Island**, which in 1773 was called St Kitts Island. But why such a connection was made – unless as a joke – is unknown.

❧ BROAD HINTON

This was plain Hentone in the Domesday Book. The spelling Brodehenton first appears in 1319. This Saxon name means the large heahtun (high settlement).

Nearby **Bincknoll Castle** derives from the Saxon words beona (bees) cnoll (small hill). The word 'castle' probably refers to an earth and wood motte and bailey castle built here after the Norman Conquest.

Uffcott was Ufecote in the Domesday Book and means the cot (cottage) of Uffa. **Conegar Copse** refers to rabbits.

❧ BROCKENBOROUGH

When this name was first recorded in 956 it was in the form brokene berrege. It did not achieve a more recognisable form – Brokenburgh – until 1232. The name is Saxon, meaning the broken barrow. The reference may be to a ruined burial mound. Alternatively, the word 'beorg' may mean hill. There is some evidence to suggest that originally the place had a Welsh name something like Caerduro.

Twatley Farm may mean the look-out clearing from Saxon 'tote' and 'leah'. It was first recorded in 956 as Tothele. **Bell Farm** may refer to a field shape as it appears in the Tithe Award for 1840 as Bell End. **Boakley Farm** means the leah (clearing) of the beech trees, while **Fosse Farm** takes its name from the nearby Roman road, the Fosse Way.

A particularly intriguing name is that of **Gilboa Farm**, but why it should have taken its name from the Old Testament site is a mystery.

❧ BROMHAM

Called Bromham in the Domesday Book, the name means the hamm (land in the bend of a river), where broom grows. In place-name studies the Saxon word hamm can be confused with another word, ham (village). Early spellings are needed to tell the words apart. Bromham is on the Clackers Brook, a small tributary of the river Avon. This makes it more likely that it contains hamm, than ham. The grave of the poet, Tom Moore, is marked by a large Irish cross in the churchyard of St Nicholas's church.

Hawk Street Farm was Hauekestret in 1288 and probably preserves a family name.

Nether Street dates from at least 1288. It means the lower street, probably used in the sense of strung-out settlement.

Oliver's Castle takes its name from Oliver Cromwell, and arises from a tradition of a battle fought here in the Civil War. The same tradition gave rise to the name of nearby **Bloody Battle Ditch**. Oliver's Castle itself is a hill fort covering some 1.2ha and enclosed within a single bank and ditch. Excavations here produced early Iron Age pottery. There are also two Bronze Age bowl barrows within the fort, one of which produced a bronze dagger accompanying a cremation burial.

St Edith's Marsh was originally Edithelegh (Edith's clearing) in 1374. The reference to 'saint' does not appear until 1569.

Clay Barn takes its name from the local soil which gave rise to Cleystret

(1354), Cleyfeld (1377), le South Cley and North Cley (1564), Upper Cley and Lower Cley (1840).

✖ BROUGHTON GIFFORD

This name is from the Saxon broctun (stream settlement); it was Broctun in 1001. The second part is from John Giffard, who owned land here in 1281.

Challymead House, first mentioned in 1525 as Chaldmede, takes its name from a Saxon field-name meaning cold meadow. A rather more attractive version of the name is found in the form Cherrymead recorded in 1773 but this form disguises the real meaning.

Chessells, a field name in the village, was Chesselfreth in 1642. The older name refers to an old wood there as it is derived from the Saxon word fyrhthe (wood). Chessell may be from the Saxon cisel (gravel), referring to the quality of the soil.

Hollybrook House refers to an area taking its name from the brook in the hollow, rather than from the tree.

Monkton House stands on the site of Monkton, first recorded in 1325 and meaning the tun (settlement) of the monks. The land belonged to the priory at Monkton Farleigh.

✖ BULFORD

This name has nothing to do with bulls. It means the ford where the plant ragged robin grows. What sounds today like bull, is in fact derived from the Saxon word bulut, for ragged robin, or cuckoo flower. In 1178 it was called Bultisford, though it had been shortened to Bultford by 1341 and to Bulford by the early 17th century. Just north of Bulford the kiwi cut in the side of Beacon Hill was the work of New Zealand troops stationed there in the First World War.

Local legend claims that a large stone, lying in the river Avon at Bulford, was dropped by the Devil as he was taking it to build Stonehenge. This legend is clearly influenced by the realisation that pagan worship took place at Stonehenge and similar traditions are linked to other isolated large stones in the county. The stone has now been removed from the Avon and is actually made of limestone and is not one of the sarsens, or bluestones, which went into the building of Wiltshire's most famous prehistoric monument.

❧ BULKINTON

This is Bulca's farm and was first recorded in the Domesday Book as Bolintone. A more representative spelling – Bolkintone – appears in 1211. **Shortmarsh Lane** in the village takes its name from a field-name recorded on the Tithe Map of 1840.

❧ BURBAGE

The name was first mentioned in 961, as Burgbeces. It means the burg (fort) on the ridge. The second part of the name is the Saxon word baec, meaning back. The mention of an 'eorthburh' (earthfort) in a Saxon charter for Burbage suggests that there was a fort there.

Nearby **Bowden Farm** is first mentioned in 1626 and may be derived from the Saxon word boga (curve) referring to the shape of the rounded hill it is sited on.

Ladywell Copse actually finds its origin in the Saxon word hlaedel (ladle) and probably refers to a means for getting water from the well.

❧ BURCOMBE

First recorded in 937 as Brydancumb the name probably means Bryda's cumb (short, broad valley). The alternative is the cumb of the bryd (bride) but it is difficult to see what this could have meant.

Nearby **Burcombe Ivers** is the yfer (slope) of Burcombe. It refers to the chalk downland.

Ugford was Ucganford in 956 and means the ford of Ucga. It has over the years also had the alternative names of Uggeford St Jacques (1382) and Ugforde Abbesse (1544).

❀ BUTTERMERE

Recorded in 863 as Butermere, the meaning is the butter mere (pond). **Henley** was henna leah in 961 and means hen leah (clearing). **Rockmoor** probably does not refer to rocks but to a dialect word 'drock' meaning a small ditch, or drain.

·· C ··

❀ CALNE

The name has been spelled this way since 955. It means the loud river and comes from the Welsh word ceiliog, related to the Latin calare (to call, shout). The present town-name was therefore originally the name of the river which is now called the Abberd Brook. The name reminds us that had it not been for the Anglo-Saxon settlement of England in the Dark Ages, Wiltshire would now be Welsh speaking.

Doctor's Pond is named after Joseph Priestley, who discovered oxygen. He is said to have collected gases from water bubbles here. Both **Silver Street** (first recorded 1649) and **Wood Street** (first recorded 1232) preserve memories of goods once sold there. The **Lansdowne Arms** pub was originally the Catherine Wheel, though in a mid 17th century change of name – prompted by Puritan desires to remove references to a saint, the veneration of whom they considered superstition – it became the Cat and Wheel.

Bowood House, now a stately home open to the public, is derived from a Saxon original, bufanwuda (above the wood). The house is the home of the Earl and Countess of Shelburne. The great picture gallery in the house was originally an orangery, designed by Robert Adam. It was in Bowood House that Dr Priestley had the laboratory where he worked on his discovery of oxygen. The estate is now also home to a very large children's adventure playground and an 18 hole championship golf course.

Calstone Wellington links a Saxon name – Calne tun (settlement) – with the name of a 13th century landowner, Ralph de Wilinton. **Chilvester** is

Saxon for calf wooded-hill; the second element being the word hyrst.

Horsley appears to mean hors leah (horse clearing) and derive from two common Saxon words. However a spelling of 1279 – Horsliperith – shows it actually means horse-slip! It must refer to a slippery place where a horse would find it difficult to keep its footing.

Quemerford probably contains the Welsh word cymmer (confluence of streams) to which has been added the Saxon word ford. **Pilpot Wood** was Filpott Coppice in 1650 and the reference to 'filling the pot' may suggest it was a productive and useful area of land.

Stockley is from the two Saxon words stocc (stump) leah (clearing). The same word survives in **Stock Street**.

At nearby **Studley**, which is the horse clearing – the first element being the original of the modern word stud – is the **Soho** pub. It takes its name not from the area of London but from a hunting cry.

❧ CANNINGS (ALL and BISHOPS)

This is a type of place-name rare in Wiltshire. It is derived from a Saxon name Caningas, meaning the people of Cana. The word 'ingas' (people of…) refers to a group of settlers named after their leader, or ancestor. Names formed from this normally end in 'ing' (eg Reading) but Cannings is one of the few examples nationally where the 's' from the word ingas has survived; another example is Hastings, in Sussex. At one time it was thought that ingas place-names were the earliest English place-names. More recent research has shown that this is not the case but they still date from early in the Anglo-Saxon period. **All Cannings** is from Saxon ealdan (old). **Bishops Cannings** was a manor of the diocese of Salisbury. It was first mentioned in the *Anglo-Saxon Chronicle* in 1010 as Canegan. According to legend it was at Bishops Cannings that local smugglers pretended to revenue men that they were raking in the moon from the local pond instead of barrels of contraband, thus earning citizens of Wiltshire the name of 'moonrakers'.

Bourton is the burgtun (fortified settlement) and may refer to a defended manor house. **Calcote Farm** is from the Saxon for cold cottage. **Easton Farm** is Saxon for the east settlement.

✱ CASTLE COMBE

The original name – Combe – simply meant the short, broad valley, from the single Saxon word cumb. The fact that a Norman castle was built here caused the name to be changed during the Middle Ages. In the Domesday Book it was just plain Come, but by 1270 it had become Castelcumbe. The tomb of Walter de Dunstanville, who built the castle, can be found in the parish church. The village was chosen as the unlikely setting for a seaside port in the film *Dr Doolittle*.

Shrub House was la Schrubbe in 1354, derived from a Middle English word for overgrown land. **East Combe Farm** was originally named Overcombe and appears by this name in 1453.

Castle Combe

❧ CHALKE, BOWER and BROAD

The modern name sounds more like its meaning that the original spelling of 826 – Cealcan. It is quite simply chalk downland, from the Saxon word cealc, indicating both chalk and limestone. Bower is from Saxon burg, meaning in this case borough, rather than fort. Broad is from Saxon brad (important). The spelling Chalke appears from the mid 13th century. Local legend claims that a golden coffin is buried somewhere on Bowerchalk Down. According to tradition it was stolen from a nearby ancient barrow. The same legend claims that seven men may be seen dragging the coffin across the downs. The implication is that they are cursed for digging it up in the first place and this kind of belief is similar to those associated with legends of curses affecting excavators of Egyptian pyramids.

Gurston, near Broad Chalke, means Gerard's tun (settlement) and takes its name from a 12th century landowner. In this case the Saxon word tun was still being used well after the Norman Conquest.

Knighton means the tun (settlement) of the cnihts (household servants). The Saxon word cniht developed into the more illustrious 'knight'.

Little London is a humorous name for a distant corner of the parish and is similar to other names such as Scotland and Ireland which are found elsewhere.

The proximity of the county boundary helps explain the unusually named **Shire Rack**. It actually means the shire oak. **Stoke Farthing** comes from the Saxon word stoc (outlying farm) and the name of a 13th century landowner, not the coin! **Vernditch** shows a Wiltshire dialect shift of 'f' to 'v'. It actually means fern ditch and in the 13th century the name was spelled Ferndich.

❧ CHAPMANSLADE

This name – first spelled Chepmanslade in 1396 – means the peddlars' short valley, from Saxon ceapman (pedlar) and slaed. Slaed is more common in field-names and charters than in place-names.

Nearby **Black Dog Wood** and **Black Dog Farm** take their names from a coaching inn on the Warminster–Bath road, now the A36. **Five Lords Farm** is so named because it is on the meeting point of the boundaries of five manors.

❦ CHARLTON (near MALMESBURY)

Derived from the Saxon name ceorltun, it means the settlement of the free peasants. This one was first recorded in a charter dating from 680 as Cherletune and is a very early record indeed. There are four Charltons, one near Malmesbury, another near Pewsey and two near Salisbury. The fact that there are a number of these names in Wiltshire led to this example being briefly called Cherleton juxta Malmesbury in 1289. This appeared again in 1523 as Chorelton juxta Malmesburye.

Kings Hay has nothing to do with monarchs but takes its name from a Saxon personal name Cynegar and tun (settlement).

Lipe Farm is derived from the Saxon word hlype (steep slope). **Pink Lane Farm** dates from at least the 13th century and probably is derived from a personal-name, or nickname.

Swatnage Wood may mean the sweet hedge and refer to flower growing in the hedge. It dates from at least the 13th century.

❦ CHARLTON (near PEWSEY)

In 1302 this was called Churleton next Upavon, to tell it apart from the other Charltons in Wiltshire. This Charlton is home to the **Charlton Cat** public house. It was originally called the Poore's Arms but a sign painter's attempt to draw the leopard on the coat of arms made it look more like a cat. Local humour caused the name to change.

❦ CHERHILL

The 1155 spelling Ciriel makes it clear that the second element in the name is the Welsh word ial (uplands), also found in the place-name Deverill. The first element may be the Welsh word caer (fortress), a reference to a hillfort.

Gores Plantation probably contains an old field-name. The Saxon word gara meant a triangular piece of land left after a pattern of ploughed furrows had been laid out.

Oldbury Castle hillfort is literally the old burg (fort) and comes from two Saxon words.

❧ CHEVERELL (GREAT and LITTLE)

Possibly roebuck, from Old French chevreuil, or it may contain the Saxon plant name chervil. In the Domesday Book it was Chevrel. Great Cheverell was Chiverel Magna and Little Cheverell was Chiverel Parva in 1242.

Henning Wood near Great Cheverell is actually a corruption of Hanging Wood and was so-called in 1797.

❧ CHICKLADE

This name is one of a small number in Wiltshire where a Welsh and a Saxon word are combined to construct one place-name. This may indicate that the place had a pre-Saxon name to which has been added a Saxon one, or that a pre-Saxon word entered the vocabulary of the early Anglo-Saxon settlers. In this case the two words are the British ceto, Welsh coed (wood) and the Saxon hlid (gate). It first appeared in 912 in the form Cytlid, by 1232 it had developed into Chicled and in 1279 appeared in the very recognisable version Chikkelade.

What is now called **Great Ridge** was in 1348 originally named Chicladrygh (Chicklade ridge).

Bockerley Hill may derive from the Saxon bocleah (beech wood). In this case leah may have been used with its older meaning of 'wood', rather than in the sense 'clearing'. This last meaning is one that developed in the later Anglo-Saxon period.

❧ CHILMARK

The pole on the boundary, from the Saxon words cigel (pole) and mearc (boundary). It refers to a boundary marker. The name was first spelled Cigel marc in 984. By Domesday Book this had become Chilmerc. Stone from Chilmark went into the building of Salisbury Cathedral. **Fricker Lane** takes its name from a family named Fryker, who lived in the vicinity in the 1570s.

Chilmark Down was originally North Downe (1695). **Cleeve Copse** probably contains the Saxon word clif (cliff, steep slope). **Hart Coppice** possibly refers to deer but alternatively may arise from the shape of the wood. This could be why the name was spelled Heart Coppice in 1820, although it may be a corruption of the original spelling.

Mooray has an interesting origin. It comes from the Saxon word morgengifu (morning gift). This was a gift (of land, in this and many cases) made by a husband to his wife on the morning after their marriage.

🌸 CHIPPENHAM

A Saxon name, it means Cippa's hamm (land in the bend of a river). The river in question is the Avon. The place was first mentioned in the *Anglo-Saxon Chronicle*, which tells how in the winter of 878 the Vikings almost captured King Alfred here. Chippenham later became an important market town. Legend has it that **Maud Heath's Causeway** was built to provide a safe path from Wick Hill to the town. Maud Heath, a wealthy landowner, lived in 1474 at Langley Burrell. Some of the street names are very old. **Bath Road** was Batheweye in 1300, **Emery Lane** was Ymbri in 1314. **The Shambles** was the site of the old market and comes from the Saxon word scamol (animal pen).

Sheldon is Saxon and means the scylf (shelf) dun (hill). The reference is probably to a slope. **Sheldon Manor** is now famous as a fine country house.

Tytherton Lucas, **East Tytherton** both derive from a Saxon name meaning the tun (settlement) of Tiedre. Lucas refers to the landowner in 1249.

Nearby farm names include **Allington** from Aelle's tun (settlement); **Cheverden** from cefer (beetle) denu (hill); **Derriads** from deor (animal) geard (enclosure); **Fowlswick** from Fugol's wic (dairy farm); **Shipway's Farm** from schepwashe (sheep-wash). All are Saxon names.

❧ CHIRTON

This village takes its name from a Saxon original ciricetun (church village). Nearby **Conock** is a Welsh name but its meaning here is not clear.

❧ CHISLEDON

In 880 this was Cyseldene and means, in the Saxon language, the ciseldenu (gravel valley). **Butts Road** probably refers to medieval archery and **High Street** has carried this name since at least 1608. The Bronze Age bowl barrow in **Gypsy Lane** is one of a number of Wiltshire barrows which legend insists contains a golden coffin. The legend here claimed that attempts to excavate the barrow were thwarted by tools breaking or some other interruption. Also the tree atop the barrow was – in the same legend – supposed to be unique in some way.

Nearby **Burderop** takes its name from an ancient fortification and means the burg (fort) thorp (hamlet). The second element is common in the Midlands and north, areas of Viking settlement.

Hodson comes from Hodd's tun (settlement), while **Snowshill** is Snodd's hill, not a reference to wintry weather.

❧ CHITTERNE

A mix of Saxon and Welsh words, Chitterne means house in the forest, from British ceto, Welsh coed (wood) and Saxon aern (house). It was spelled Chetre in the Domesday Book. **Chitterne St Mary** was called Cettre Beate Marie in 1291 and Chitterne Maiden in 1325.

❧ CHITTOE

A very old name, this is probably derived from the British/Welsh words ceto/coed (wood) and yw (yew). In 1167 it was spelled Chetewe.

Brogbrook reveals an interesting shift of sounds from 'f' to 'b'. In the late 16th century it was Froggebrooke. **Spye Park** probably refers to its high position.

✤ CHOLDERTON

First recorded in the Domesday Book as Celdretone. It means the settlement of Ceol, a Saxon personal name. The prehistoric Devil's Ditch north of Cholderton is also called Grim's Ditch, from a Saxon name for the pagan god Woden.

Scotland may arise from the Saxon word sceat, referring to land on the edge of an estate but is probably a joking reference to a distant part of the parish.

✤ CHRISTIAN MALFORD

This name means ford marked by a cross, from the Saxon words cristel-mael and ford. This meaning is clear from a spelling of the name in 937 when it was called Cristemaleford.
Nearby **Dodford Farm** is first mentioned in 1255 as Dodeford and is derived from the Saxon Dodda's ford.

✤ CHUTE

The village takes its name from an area of medieval forest. This in turn is derived from the British word ceto which became the modern Welsh word coed and means forest. It is a survival of a place-name that existed before the Anglo-Saxon settlements in the Dark Ages. This meaning is clear from a spelling of 1235 which is in the form Cett. North of the Roman road tradition claims there once lay a stone called the **Kinwardstone**. This was supposed to be the stone of a Saxon named Kinward and served as the meeting place of the administrative district known as the Hundred of Kinwardstone. In fact the name of the Hundred – first recorded in the Exeter version of the Domesday Book as Cheneuuarestan – takes its name from Cyneweard's stone and the meeting place was near the modern **Kinwardstone Farm**. The stone itself had a number of legends associated with it. One was that it was the Devil's waistcoat, another that the wavy lines on it were once the entrails of a man. Yet another is that one attempt to move the stone ended when the horse pulling at it dropped dead. The stone is no longer there and was probably moved to make way for modern farm machinery.

Nearby **Shaw Farm** is from the Saxon word sceaga which means a small wood. **Standen** is the stan (stoney) denu (large valley). It probably takes its name from the sarsen boulders in the vicinity. The farm name **New Zealand** is one of that fairly common class of names used for a remote settlement.

❀ CLARENDON

Probably clover hill, from Saxon claefre (clover) and dun (hill). In 1130 it was called Clarendona, very similar to the modern spelling. The medieval royal palace here was greatly enlarged in the reigns of Henry II and Henry III and it benefited from its site within a royal hunting forest. This was a very popular residence with royalty in the Middle Ages and was built for comfortable living. It covered about 6 acres and many important royal decrees were issued from here, including the Constitution of Clarendon (1164) and the Assize of Clarendon (1166). One of Edward II's parliaments met here in 1317, Edward III's eldest daughter was born here in 1331 and in 1356 the hostage kings of France and Scotland were brought here after suffering defeat at the hands of the English. The strange fact is that little now remains of this palace. Above ground there is only a fragment of walling and the site is overgrown with trees.

Nearby **Chesel** comes from a Saxon name cisleah, meaning gravel clearing. **Dogkennel Farm** was first recorded as such in 1650. It was probably a joking reference to a small house.

❀ CLYFFE PYPARD

This name – which first appeared in 983 as Clife – means quite simply the steep slope. The second part of the name records the name of a 13th century landowner. **Bushton** is the Bishop's settlement and was owned by the Bishop of Winchester.

The oddly named **The Mermaid** probably is a corruption of a Saxon word gemaere (boundary). **Nebo Farm** takes its name from a place mentioned in the Bible. This may be because the farm is situated on an upland site like the Biblical place. The theme is continued in a nearby piece of land called **Jericho Field**.

❧ CODFORD

Nothing to do with fish, the name is derived from the Saxon name Coda's ford. In 901 it was Codanford. **Codford St Peter** and **Codford St Mary** are named from their parish churches. That of Codford St Peter is famous for a magnificent Anglo-Saxon carving of a dancing man. Who the man represents is a mystery.

❧ COLERNE

The Domesday Book and modern spellings of this name are identical. It means charcoal house, from Saxon col (coal) and aern (house). Col is often used of charcoal, as well as coal. In this place the former meaning is more likely.

Danes Tump takes its name from a local tradition that a Viking king is buried there. This is typical of a number of Wiltshire legends which claim that prehistoric – often Bronze Age – burial mounds are the graves of kings.

Nearby **Doncombe** means Dunna's valley, after a Saxon landowner. The unusually named **The Ripples** derives from a Saxon word rippel (strip of land) and was recorded as Repelis in 1363. **Eastrip** is Saxon, meaning the ash-tree hamlet. **Euridge Farm** means the yew ridge and first appears in 1156 as Ewerigga.

❧ COLLINGBOURNE (DUCIS and KINGSTON)

The stream of the people living on the river Coll, from a Welsh river-name 'Coll' (meaning hazel trees) and the Saxon word burna (stream). This river-name was probably the earlier name of the upper course of what is now the river Bourne. Ducis was held by the Dukes of Lancaster, Kingston indicates it was a royal manor. In 903 the name was Colengaburnam.

At Collingbourne Ducis is **Hougomont Farm** which takes its name from a farm fought over during the battle of Waterloo in 1815.

At Collingbourne Kingston is **Aughton** which is Aeffe's tun (settlement);

Brunton, the haematun (village of the people) by the burg (fort) and **Sunton**, the south haematun (village of the people).

❀ COMPTON BASSETT

At the time of the writing of the Domesday Book in 1086, this was plain Contone and derives from two Saxon words, cumb (short, broad valley) and tun (settlement). Bassett comes from Fulke Basset who owned land here in the 13th century.

Nolands Farm probably means the old land, which would refer to land once cultivated but later abandoned. **Freeth Farm** contains the Saxon word fyrthe (wooded countryside).

Horn Wood is probably a reference to its shape. **Starve Knoll** refers to disappointing land and is similar to the name Starveall, instances of which appear throughout Wiltshire.

❀ COMPTON CHAMBERLAYNE

Identical in meaning to the other Wiltshire Compton, the distinguishing second part is from the name of a 13th century landholder here.

Naishes Farm comes from the Middle English for ash tree.

❀ COOMBE BISSETT

Plain Come in the Domesday Book, the name derives from the Saxon word cumb (short, broad valley). Bissett is from a 12th century landowner.

Coombe Bissett Bridge was ponte de Cumbe in 1249. **Coombe Bissett Down** was montem de Cumbe in 1279. Both are Latin versions of the modern names. The chalk downland on Coombe Bissett Down was saved in 1996 as an important natural heritage site. It is one of only 25 sites in the country where the rare burnt orchid can be found. The best time of the year to enjoy the down's profusion of wild flowers is between March and September. The cowslips are particularly striking as they grow here in huge numbers.

✻ CORSHAM

First recorded in 1001 as Coseham, it is an Anglo-Saxon name meaning Cosa's ham (village). The early Saxon word 'ham' is fairly rare in Wiltshire. Usually the slightly later Saxon word 'tun' was used to describe settlements in Wiltshire. The town grew rich on the weaving trade and in High Street there survive both large Georgian houses, built by clothiers, and smaller weavers' cottages. **The Methuen Arms**, named after a local family of clothiers, was the Red Lion Inn in 1809 and is on the site of a house called Winters Court, which stood here in the early 15th century.

The Saxon name **Gastard** means something like goat-land and first appears in the 12th century as Gatesterta.

Hartham derives from a Saxon form heort hamm and means deer enclosure. In this example the word hamm is used of an enclosure rather than its usual meaning of land in the bend of a river (ie 'enclosed' by water).

Neston means tun (settlement) on a naess headland and describes its hilltop site; a feature obviously noticeable to its first Saxon owners. **Pickwick** comes from two Saxon words, pic (point) and wic (dairy farm), thus linking a landscape feature with its agricultural use.

Thingley combines two words. One is the familiar Saxon word leah (clearing); the other is a word common in areas of Viking settlement, thing (assembly). It may be that this is a loan word from Danish, or perhaps that there was a similar Saxon word. Either way it suggests that this was a communal meeting place.

✻ CORSLEY

The name combines Welsh cors (reeds, bog) with Saxon leah (clearing). In the Domesday Book it was Corselie.

Cley Hill is a striking outcrop of upper chalk and stands dramatically to one side of the Warminster bypass. The name would suggest a hill with clay soil. However, the chalk makes this unlikely and its meaning is uncertain. It is topped by a prominent mound which functioned as the site of a beacon. Nearby is the smaller Little Cley Hill; hence the local rhyme 'Big Cley Hill do wear a hat, Little Cley Hill do laugh at that!'

Sturford means the steer ford and is derived from the Saxon word steor. Rather mysterious is **Mad Doctor's Farm,** first recorded as such in 1773 but the origin is unknown.

❀ CRICKLADE

As with a number of Wiltshire place-names this one mixes Saxon and Welsh words. It means the crossing place by the hill, from Welsh cruc (hill) and Saxon gelad (a crossing, or passage). The reference is clearly to a crossing point on the river Thames. The combination of the two different languages is clear in the earliest spelling (from 905), Crecca gelad. Coins minted here before the Norman Conquest however show that there were many different spellings: Croci, Crocglad, Crecela and Creccelad to name just a few of the variations! **Horse Fair Lane** in the town has been called this since at least 1633, when it was Horsfayre lane.

Bournelake Farm comes from the Saxon words burna (stream) and lacu (lake), though in 1773 it appeared in the striking spelling Bone Lick!

Calcutt is derived from the Saxon Cola's cot (cottage). **Chelworth,** another Saxon name, is from Ceol's worth (farmstead). **Dudgemore Farm** takes its name from Dudd's mere (lake, pond).

The unusually named **The Forty** was also the name of Nicholas de la Fortye, who owned land there in 1281. In fact he took his name from the place rather than the other way round, as Forty derives from a Saxon original, fortheg (literally meaning forward-island and referring to land jutting into marshland).

Gospel Oak Farm undoubtedly takes its name from the ancient beating of the parish bounds and would have been one of the places where a passage of the Bible was read during the perambulation. It is recorded as early as 1553, in the form Gospell oke.

Hailstone Farm may indeed be named from the weather, or alternatively take its name from the Saxon words halig stan (holy stone), perhaps referring to pagan worship.

Widhill has carried this name since at least 1086, when it appears in the Domesday Book as Widehille. The meaning is hill where withys grow.

❊ CRUDWELL

First mentioned in a charter of 854 as Croddewell, the name is Saxon and means Creoda's well. The modern spelling first makes an appearance in 1624 when the place was called West Crudwell. Interestingly, the place has also been called Estcruddewell (1345) and Chirche Crudwell (1624) at various points in its long history.

Chedglow is called Chegeslei in the Domesday Book; it suggests gorse covered burial mound, from the Saxon words ceacge (gorse) and hlaew, but the word hlaew can also mean small, round hill. Recorded in 1220 there is a Cheggeberewe, again meaning gorse hill but using the Saxon word beorg for hill. So it is possible that the hlaew in Chedglow means small, round hill, not burial mound.

Chelworth is the worth (homestead) of Ceolla and is Saxon. **Eastcourt** is first recorded in 901 and means the east cottages. **Flisteridge Wood** probably contains the Saxon word for fleece, referring to sheep-keeping. **Murcott** takes its name from morcot (cottage by the marsh).

❊ DAUNTSEY

Derived from the Saxon Domgeat's ieg (island), the word for island is in the West Saxon dialect, the usual Saxon word being 'eg'. It usually means dry ground in a marsh. In 850 it was Dameteseye and in the Domesday Book the spelling was Dantesie.

Idover Farm is from a Welsh stream-name. First recorded in 850, it is probably derived from ywdwfr (yew stream). **Smithcot Farm** appears in Domesday Book as Smitecote, the smith's cottage and is a Saxon name. **Waite Hill Farm** means look-out hill, from Middle English waite (watch).

❊ DEAN, WEST

A Saxon name, this was Deone in 880 and comes from the word denu, meaning large valley. The addition of 'West' is to differentiate it from another Dean, in Hampshire.

Nearby **Bentley Wood** is the beonet (bentgrass) leah (clearing). The first – and rather odd – Saxon word is found in a number of English place-names and may have referred to particularly tall grass.

Highwood Copse is probably not a reference to its height but to the fact that it was enclosed. This would then make the original the Saxon word gehaeg (enclosure), from which the modern word hedge is derived.

❧ DEVERILL (BRIXTON, HILL, KINGSTON, LONGBRIDGE, and MONKTON)

A number of villages south of Warminster share this unusual name. It means river in the fertile uplands, from the Welsh dwfrial. This derivation is based on a reference to the area in 968 as Defereal, or Deferael. In the 11th century all the settlements along the valley were included in the same general name. The distinguishing names are mostly Saxon.

Brixton Deverill is Beorhtsige's tun (settlement). **Whitecliff Farm** takes its name from a steep slope also sometimes called Whitley (white clearing, or wood) in the past. **Cold Kitchen Hill** refers to domestic rubbish dumped here. **Langley Farm** comes from the long leah (clearing), the same Saxon word found in Whitley.

Hill Deverill is from the Saxon word hyll (hill). This word was often used of a hill less rounded than one described by the word 'dun'. This place is much shrunken from its medieval size and abandoned earthwork remains of former properties can be traced on the ground here.

Kingston Deverill is from cyninges (king's) tun (settlement). **Holcombe** means the deep valley. **Marcombe** is the valley on the gemaere (a Saxon word meaning boundary). Both contain the Saxon word cumb, a word often used for valleys shorter and broader than described by the word 'denu', but here used for a deeper dip in the landscape.

Longbridge Deverill is first recorded as Longo ponte in 1252. **Crockerton** means the tun (settlement) of the potters and takes its name from the medieval word crokker (potter). The close proximity of **Potter's Hill**

is noteworthy. **Shute Farm** indicates a corner of land, while **Swan-combe Bottom** has nothing to do with swans but instead indicates the place where swine were kept.

Monkton Deverill is the tun (settlement) of the monks and belonged to Glastonbury Abbey in the Domesday Book. **Boar's Bottom** is derived from a local family name. Near Monkton Deverill is the Pertwood Down long barrow. This survivor from the New Stone Age is some 79m long, with a distinct gap between the ditch and mound.

🦋 DEVIZES

This name means 'the boundaries'. Unlike most Wiltshire place-names it is not Saxon but French. In 1139 it was Divisas. The boundary in the name is that of the hundreds of Potterne and Cannings. It is one of the very few names in England coined by the Normans, who usually took over existing names. A castle was built here in 1120 and the line of its defences can still be traced in some of the modern roads such as **Monday Market Street**. Not surprisingly this takes its name from one of the town's medieval markets. The churches of St John's and St Mary's are Norman and the town also has some fine 15th century houses and larger buildings like the Queen's Head and the Black Swan, which date from the 18th century. The unusual name **The Brittox** dates from 1300 and means a fortified place. It was probably inspired by the nearby castle walls. An inscription on the cornmarket cross tells the story of Ruth Pierce of Potterne who claimed she had paid for wheat at the market and swore she would drop dead if lying. She repeated the oath and did drop dead, the money clutched in her hand.

The history of the area and the county is displayed in the museum of the Wiltshire Archaeological and Natural History Society. This fine building is located in Long Street and contains a huge range of artifacts from the county's world-famous sites.

Nearby village names are Saxon including **Potterne** meaning the potters' aern (hut); **Marston**, the marsh tun (settlement); Rowde from hreod (place where reeds grow).

Wallen Lane, in Potterne, means land of the weala (Welsh). This Saxon word refers to British people living here when the first Anglo-Saxon settlers arrived in the area.

The name of the hillfort **Oliver's Castle** refers to the 17th century parliamentary leader. According to local legend the site is haunted by the ghosts of Roundhead cavalry slaughtered at the battle of Roundway Down (1643). The hillfort is also the reputed hiding place of treasure. This is supposed to be in the form of a golden coffin. Incidentally Oliver Cromwell had nothing to do with this hillfort! The parliamentary commander at Roundway Down was Sir William Waller and this is an example of how local traditions can sometimes be very imaginative in their handling of historical data and should be treated with caution.

❈ DILTON MARSH

First recorded as Dulintun in 1190, this Saxon name means Dylla's tun (settlement). The addition of Marsh is later and self explanatory. It is recorded as Mersshe in 1332.

The **Prince of Wales** pub is named not from the modern holder of the title but from Edward II, who was created the first Prince of Wales in 1301. The area known as **Stormore** is first recorded with that name in 1606, in a reference to a small patch of woodland. The name may be an abbreviation and refer to moorland (waste land) owned by the manor of Stourton. Nearby **Chalcot House** is the site of a 17th century manor house which stands on the site of a medieval building, itself close to a Roman settlement. The present house was built in about 1680 of brick with stone dressings. Altered in both the 18th and the 19th centuries, it was restored in the 1970s and won a European Architectural Heritage Award.

At **Old Dilton** the church of St Mary has 14th and 15th century external features, while inside Georgian woodwork, a three-decker pulpit and plain panelled box pews make a visit to this church memorable.

Bremeridge Farm takes its name from the Saxon word bremel (bramble), while the name of **Chalcot House** is first recorded in 1249 and is derived from the Saxon cealdcot (cold cottages)

Short Street probably derives from shoot and refers to medieval archery in the area.

❄ DINTON

This is Dunna's tun (settlement) and named from an otherwise unknown Saxon landowner. The present name is a contraction of the original, as in the Domesday Book it was Domnitone and in 1184 Duninton. The use of the Saxon place-name forming element 'ingtun' means settlement of the person whose name is linked to the place. When the element is in the plural – ingatun – it means 'settlement of the people of...' In the case of Dinton the early spellings show it to be a name formed from ingtun rather than from ingatun. The village contains no less than four National Trust properties: Hyde's House, reputedly the birthplace of Edward Hyde, Earl of Clarendon; Lawes Cottage, the 17th century home of the composer William Lawes; Little Clarendon, a 15th century building; Philipps House, built in 1814-17 for William Wyndham and famous for its huge portico with Ionic columns and pediment and an impressive central staircase built from Portland stone.

Dalwood Farm is the dell wood, meaning the wood in a tiny valley. The Saxon word dell is usually only found in minor names and in field-names.

Other nearby minor names include **Marshwood Farm** which first appears as Merswode in 1276; **Oakley**, the oak leah (clearing); **Snapes**, a small patch of land; and **Swindley Copse** meaning pig clearing.

❄ DONHEAD (ST ANDREW, ST MARY)

Spelled Dunheued, in 871, it means top of the hill, from the Saxon words dun (hill) and heafod (head). The combination of elements and the location of Donhead St Mary suggests that the meaning is a jutting shelf of land below a hill summit.

Donhead St Andrew takes its name from its church dedication and this first appears in 1298 in the form Sancti Andree de Dunheved. It was also alternatively called Nether Donhead and appears – in the form Nether Donet – in 1618. **Arundell Farm** takes its name from the owners of Wardour Castle. **Nower's Copse** probably derives from the Saxon word ora (bank).

Donhead St Mary first appears with the addition of its church dedication in 1298, when it was spelled Donheved Sancte Marie. In 1618 it was alternatively called Over Donet, as another way of distinguishing it from Donhead St Andrew. **Charlton** is from the Saxon ceorlatun (settlement of the free peasants). These were the lowest class of free farmers. **Ludwell** is the loud spring. The Saxon word wiell usually meant spring, though its modern descendant is of course the word 'well'. **Tittlepath Hill** takes its name from a Saxon word sticelanpath (steep path)

✿ DOWNTON

This is derived from two Saxon words: dun (hill) and tun (settlement). The name was spelled Duntun in 672, Duntone in Domesday Book and Donton in 1290. **Watership Lane** takes its name from a Saxon word waterscipe (water conduit). The inn facing the old cross has wooden busts of King John and his queen Isabella set in niches. Local legend suggests they are copies of statues put here to commemorate the king and queen's visits to Downton in the early 13th century. Since before the Second World War Downton has been an angling centre for the Wylye, Nadder and Ebble, with the **Bull Hotel** acting as a meeting point.

Barford is either the beorcford (birch ford), or the bereford (barley ford). It is difficult to be certain. Both are Saxon names.

The name **Giant's Chair** is unusual in that it is given to a Bronze Age round barrow; most such names are attached to long barrows from the New Stone Age. This linking of a large earthwork to a giant is quite common – see the Giant's Graves at Oare and Milton Lilbourne

Wick takes its name from the Saxon word wic, which usually denotes a dairy farm. The word was borrowed from the Latin word vicus.

✿ DRAYCOT (CERNE, FITZPAINE and FOLIAT)

In the Domesday Book it was plain Draicote. This is a Saxon name meaning cot (cottage) by the draeg (steep slope). The word draeg is related to our modern word 'drag' and suggests a lot of effort was needed to get up the hill here. The second part of the name of Draycot Cerne is from Henry de Cerne who owned land here in 1228.

Draycot FitzPaine. The second part of this name is from Margery Fitz-payn who owned the manor in 1327.

Draycot Foliat. Henry Foliot owned the manor here in 1209.

Clanville means clean open land and probably refers to land clear of weeds. In 1638 it was Clanvell but the fact that the second element is from the Saxon word feld (open land) is revealed in the 1840 spelling, Clanfield.

❧ DURNFORD

This is derived from the Saxon dierne (hidden) and ford. At the time of the Domesday Book it was Darneford, though by 1158 it appeared as Durneford. It also had a number of alternative names which did not stick. These included Derneford Magna (1270), meaning 'large' and Derneford Parva (1286) meaning little! It was also briefly called Hungerford Durnford after a family of powerful landowners (the builders of Farleigh Hungerford Castle on the Somerset/Wiltshire border). In the church the pulpit is decorated with a 17th century cloth said to be made of goat's hair. There is also a chained book dating from 1562. Some of the glass in the nave window is 15th century.

Nearby **Netton** is a Saxon name meaning the settlement of the cattle. It was called Netetune in 1242 and in 1428 the form Suthneton (South Netton) briefly appeared but did not survive.

Newtown means simply the new tun (settlement) and first appeared as such in 1289, in the form Nyweton. It is probably a late example of the use of 'tun' to make a place-name and from other examples it is clear that this word continued to be used for some time after the Norman Conquest of 1066.

Ogbury Camp probably derives from oak burg (fort) and is a Saxon name for a prehistoric hillfort. **Salterton** means tun (settlement) of the sealtera (saltworkers).

❄ DURRINGTON

The settlement of Deora, from the Saxon deoringtun. The Domesday Book spelling was Derintone. If an early spelling survives in the plural 'ingatun' the meaning is 'settlement of the people of the individual named'; when in the singular 'ingtun' – 'intone' in this example – the meaning is 'settlement belonging to the individual named'. Most Wiltshire examples are of the latter type.

South of the village is the prehistoric earthwork called **Durrington Walls**. This was called Longwall in 1790. South of this is a smaller earthwork called **Woodhenge**. This is a name coined to compare it to the more famous Stonehenge, the reason being that archaeological excavation here revealed it as the site of a wooden building. This building was roofed but its central area was open to the sky. The evidence for this structure lay in the remains of six concentric rings of postholes with a bank and ditch around them. The original construction would have been about 76m in diameter. The middle of the building contained the grave of a child, though whether this represented a sacrifice or the burial of a child from a high status family is difficult to say.

Hackthorn refers to the growth of thorn bushes in the area. **Cuckoo Stone**, the name for a large sarsen stone, may be a corruption of a name based on some local, now lost, legend, since in 1790 it was called the Cuckhold Stone.

•• E ••

❄ EASTCOTT

A number of place-names mean simply the east cottages, from a Saxon original – estcot. In each case the name was probably given to a settlement which was an off-shoot from a larger one. The three in Wiltshire are **Eastcott**, probably a daughter settlement of Littleton Pannell, or perhaps Potterne; **Eastcourt**, in Crudwell parish, possibly a daughter settlement from there and **Eastcourt**, east of Burbage. Near to the last settlement is Westcourt (Westcote, 1264).

❧ EASTERTON

A similar Saxon attempt to differentiate a village by its position in relation to another settlement gave rise to Easterton. Named Esterton, in 1412 it is the easterra (eastern) tun (settlement). It is close to the first Eastcott and probably forms part of the same secondary spread of settlement.

Twentyland near Easterton probably refers to its size and means 20 acres.

❧ EASTON

Similar to the above place-names are those derived from Saxon esttun (east settlement).

Easton is a minor name east of Corsham. It was Eston in 1375. Another minor name, **Easton Down** is in Winterslow parish.

Easton Farm is in Berwick St John parish and was Estun in a charter of 956. Another **Easton Farm** is in the parish of Bishop's Cannings and was Eston in 1332.

Easton Grey is north-east of Sherston. Grey is from Johannes Greiz who owned the manor in 1242. He took his name from a place called Graye, in Normandy. In the Domesday Book the place was called Estone and in 1289 was recorded as Eston Grey.

Easton Piercy is east of Yatton Keynell. Piercy is from Peter de Estune, a tenant here in 1189. It was Estone in the Domesday Book and the much longer Eston Peres juxta Kyngton Michis in 1304.

Easton Royal is east of Milton Lilbourne and Pewsey. The name Royal denotes that the eastern part of the parish was in the royal forest of Savernake. It was Estone in the Domesday Book, Aston in 1242, Estone by Merleberge in 1241 and Estone juxta Burbache in 1324. In 1268 it was called Estone Prioris because there was a small monastic house of Austin Canons here. Nearby **Falstone Pond** is from the Saxon fealustan (fallow stone). **Godsbury** is Saxon, first appearing in 921 in the form Guthredesburg and means Guthred's fort. It is an interesting example both of how some modern names are extreme contractions of their original form and how difficult it would be to establish the meaning of a name if one only had the modern spelling to go on. Clearly the use of early spellings is crucial if we want to make an accurate assessment of the meaning of a name.

Easton Town is a minor name in Sherston parish and was Estentowne in the 16th century.

❧ EBBESBORNE WAKE

This was Eblesburnan in 826 and comes from the Saxon Ebbel's burna (stream). Wake is from Galfridus Wac who owned the manor in 1166.

Fifield Bavant means the five hides, a Saxon unit of land. Bavant is from Roger de Bavent who owned land here in 1316. Double this amount of land gave rise to the name Tinhead, near Edington. It was Fifhide in the Domesday Book, Fifhyde juxta Eblesbourne in 1345 and Fiffehyde Beaufaunt in 1436. By 1510 this had become a more recognisable Fufhed Bavent. Interestingly enough in 1567 it appears in the form Fifield alias Fyfhed, in which the first part of the name is identical to the modern spelling but the second part has been omitted.

Chase Farm takes its name from Cranborne Chase, the medieval hunting ground which covered a large area on the Dorset-Wiltshire border.

The name of a 13th century landowner, Roger de Clyve, is preserved in the first part of **Cleeve Cottages**. The area was called just Cleeve in 1788. A much later person is remembered in **Great Bingham**. Here the name preserved is that of the rector of Berwick St John, who died in 1826.

The unusually named areas **Great** and **Little Forlorn** are nothing to do with sorrow. The 1618 version – Foure lords – gives the game away. Here is located the meeting point of four parishes – Ebbesborne, Alvediston, Berwick St John, Handley in Dorset – and it is this that gave rise to the name.

Prescombe is from the Saxon for priest's valley and indicates land belonging to the Church. **Stowford Bridge** means the stone-ford and was first recorded in 1348 as Stoforde brigge.

❧ EDINGTON

The site of the battle of Ethandune, in 878, where King Alfred of Wessex defeated the Vikings led by Guthrum. Previous to this victory Alfred had been living in the marshes of Somerset, having narrowly escaped capture by the Vikings while celebrating the previous Christmas at Chippenham. The place-name is Saxon, derived from ethedun (uncultivated hill). The first element may be the Saxon personal name Etha. The name appears as Edendone in Domesday Book and Eddington in 1546.

It is now the site of a magnificent church – St Mary, St Katherine and All Saints – which was once a priory, founded in 1362. It was from the high altar here that William Ayscough, a 15th century bishop of Salisbury, was dragged by a mob and murdered on the hill behind the church. The church is built like a small cathedral in the Perpendicular style but also combining aspects of the earlier Decorated style. There is fine medieval stained glass in the Lady Chapel and a striking double screen separates the chancel from the nave. In addition to this the building has many consecration crosses and masons' marks, as well as a 17th century pulpit and some very interesting tombs and monuments.

Edington Church

Baynton means Baega's tun (settlement) and is another Saxon name. **Ballard's Farm**, **Butler's Farm** and **Hudd's Mill** all take their names from 13th century landowners. **Court Farm** takes its name from an area of land, called Courte Close in 1550. **South Down Sleight** refers to sheep pasture and this is clear from the way it was described in 1840 as South Down Sheep Sleight.

Tinhead is from the Saxon word for ten hides, a unit of land. This would have been a significant small estate since five hides was considered sufficient to support the lowest class of Anglo-Saxon aristocratic landowner.

❧ ENFORD

Recorded in 934 as Enedford the name means duck ford and contains the Saxon word ened (duck). By 1376 it had become Endford. A large bowl barrow (a type of Bronze Age burial mound) is claimed by local legend to be the site of a buried golden chair. This bowl barrow has a diameter of about 46m and a height of 5.2m. This makes it one of the largest round barrows in Britain.

Chisenbury is the burg (fort) of the people who live on the cis (gravel). This Saxon name refers to both the quality of the local soil and a prehistoric hill fort – **Chisenbury Camp**. In the early 19th century this hillfort had the alternative name of Chisenbury Trendle, or circle.

Compton is from the Saxon cumbtun (settlement in the short, broad valley). The name first appears in the Domesday Book as Contone and in 1298 was called Compton juxta Eneford.

Fifield is another name meaning five hides (see for example **Fifield Bavant** near Ebbesborne Wake). This was enough land to support the lowest grade of Anglo-Saxon aristocrat, a thegn. It was first recorded in 1230 as Fifide, which clearly indicates its meaning. In 1310 it briefly carried the very long name of Parva Fifhide juxta Eneford, but this not surprisingly did not survive. Neither did the 1362 form Langefifhide.

New Town was new in 1773, while **Pintail Wood** is probably not a reference to the breed of duck but to the shape of the wood itself.

Slay Down has nothing to do with battles and slaughter as the name might suggest but probably contains a Saxon word meaning grassy side of a hill. It was first recorded in 1212 in the form la Slee.

❧ ERLESTOKE

This village name is derived from the Saxon eorlstoc (the earl's outlying farm). In 1239 it was called Erlestok, very similar to the modern spelling. The earl may have been Harold, the last Saxon king of England who died at the Battle of Hastings in 1066. Carvings in the church of St James include squirrels and a striking carving of a stag with a cross between its antlers and an arrow in its mouth. Local tradition claims that the more modern church of the Holy Saviour was built because the lord of the manor objected to the lower classes using 'his' church, but a fire burnt down the manor house as a punishment.

Pudnell Farm first appears in 1309 as Podenhulle and means Puda's hill. Puda was probably a Saxon landowner.

Bitham Wood contains the Saxon word bytme. This word meant something like head of a valley, or alternatively low lying ground, sometimes a place overlooking low lying ground.

❧ ETCHILHAMPTON

This is a very unusual place-name. In the Domesday Book it was called Ecesatingetone – the settlement of the people at the oak hill, from the Saxon words aechyll (oakhill) and saetingatun (settlement of the people). However, this is not the version of the name that has survived. By 1196 the name had been changed to Ehelhampton. In this version the Saxon word haematun (also meaning 'settlement of the people') had been substituted for saetingatun. Why this happened is a mystery. It is possible that the place had always had these alternative names. The complicated nature of the name is revealed in a record dating from 1622 which called the village Ashlington alias Echilhampton. Presumably Ashlington was a 17th century form of the Domesday Book name.

Etchilhampton Hill was called Ashlington Hill in the early 18th century and this probably contained a reference to ash trees.

Nearby **Tinkfield Farm** may contain the Saxon word thing (assembly) and refer to nearby **Etchilhampton Hill**, which was the meeting point of the Hundred of Cannings.

EVERLEIGH

Called Eburleagh in 704 this is Saxon for the eofor (boar) leah (clearing). The spelling Everelegh appears in 1281 and in 1563 the place was called Myddell Everley. According to local legend a well at Everleigh is supposed to have a door in the side of the well shaft. From this, it is claimed, a tunnel leads to Sidbury Hill. In the tunnel there is located a golden chair. This is similar to the legend of the golden chair supposed to be buried in the barrow at Enford. Another local tradition is that King Ine of Wessex had a palace near Everleigh. This royal connection may be behind the golden chair (throne?) legend.

Everleigh is also the location of a cemetery of Bronze Age barrows, consisting of two bell barrows, two bowl barrows and a disc barrow. These are all differently named according to their varying shapes and construction. Excavations here discovered cremated burials and the later use of the site for a pagan Anglo-Saxon burial.

Gore Down contains the Saxon word gara and refers to a triangular piece of land left over after an open field had been ploughed. Both **Milking Bushes** and **Windmill Bushes** clearly refer to the activities once practised there.

•• F ••

FARLEIGH WICK, MONKTON FARLEIGH

Both these villages take their name from a common Saxon name fearnleah (fern clearing). The first mention of the name comes from 1001 when it was spelled Farnleghe. However it is not clear which settlement was meant. Farleigh Monkton is first mentioned, in the Latinised form Monachorum, in 1316. The name indicates it was monastic land belonging to the priory here. Farlegh Wyke appears in 1365. Wick indicates that it was probably a dairy farm dependent on Monkton Farleigh. In which case the oldest settlement would be Monkton Farleigh. Inside the parish church at Monkton Farleigh is a fine 17th century pulpit. On it are carefully carved the words 'Blessed are thay yt heare ye word of God and keepe it'. The quotation is from the Gospel of St Luke, chapter 11, verse 28. In the south doorway there is a carving of a beast biting a shaft. It is typical of Romanesque sculpture which became increasingly popular in the architecture of churches during the 12th century.

Link Lane is probably a survival of the Saxon word hlinc (bank). The word also lay behind the field-names Link Mead and Great Links recorded in 1840. **Inwood Farm** was Inwodestret in 1485 and probably means the road through the wood. **Park Wood** was le Estparke in 1513, or the east park.

✿ FARLEY

First mentioned in the Domesday Book as Farlege the name is formed from two Saxon words, fearn (fern) and leah (clearing). The meaning is clearer in a reference dating from 1109 which spells the name as Fernelega. Attempts to make it clear where the place is resulted in Farlegh juxta Pitton (1285) and Farlegh juxta Claryndon (1351). The church of All Saints is an Italian Renaissance inspired building made from pink brick and dating from about 1690.

Nearby **Pitton** is from two words, putta (hawk's) and tun (settlement). Hawk may have been a personal name. **Piccadilly Clump** is probably so named because it is some distance from the heart of the parish. The reference would be to London as a measure of distance.

✿ FIGHELDEAN

This was called Fisgledene in the Domesday Book and means Fygla's denu (large valley). During its long history it has had various forms including Fykeldene (1157), Feildeane alias Fighledeane (1640) and Filedean (1718). **Ablington** is the tun (settlement) of Ealdbeald. It was Alboldintone in the Domesday Book.

Alton comes from the Saxon for Aella's tun (settlement) and was Eltone in the Domesday Book. By the 13th century this had changed to Alletona. **Choulston**, which appears in the Domesday Book as Chelestanestone, is Saxon for Ceolstan's tun (settlement). **Gallows Bridge** probably takes its name from the site of executions.

Knighton Farm is the tun (settlement) of the cnihts (serving men). This Anglo-Saxon word is the root of the medieval and modern word 'knight' but without its higher class connotations. In the Domesday Book it was spelled Wenistetone, which totally obscures its meaning, though the real origin can be discovered in later versions of the name such as Knytheton, which appears in 1270. This shows how the earliest form of a name is not always sufficient to indicate the meaning and how it is sometimes necessary to compare it with other – sometimes later – spellings.

Syrencot House. This unusual name appeared in the form Sexhamcote in 1227 and seems to mean the cottages made up of six homes.

✵ FISHERTON DE LA MERE

This has the meaning fisherman's settlement and it is located on the river Wylye near Codford. In the Domesday Book it was Fisertone. Attempts to differentiate it from Fisherton Anger, now in Salisbury, led to names such as Fisshereton juxta Wili in 1289, Fisherton juxta Codeforde in 1318 and Fyssherton Dalamare in 1412. The eventual form is derived from John de la Mare who owned the land here in 1377.

Bapton has its roots in a Saxon original called Babbington, the tun (settlement) of a man named Babba. The same personal name also appears in nearby Baverstock. This may suggest that it was the same landowner who gave his name to both estates. The fact that the present name is a contraction of the original is revealed in the spelling Babinton which appears in a record of 1221. By 1276 this has reduced to Babeton and in 1526 it appears as Bapton.

✵ FITTLETON

This is a fascinating example of how changing dialect can affect the way a name is spelled, though in this case the original name won through. It is Saxon derived from Fitela's tun (settlement). However in the Domesday Book it is spelled as Viteletone. This Domesday Book use of 'v', instead of 'f', is due to an early example of dialect pronunciation, common in later Middle English and modern south western dialects. For another example see Sutton Veny. By 1211 it was Fitletone and the 'f' remained after this.

Beach's Barn has nothing to do with the seaside. Instead it probably derives from a minor place-name called beechtree which gave rise to both this place-name and the name of a local family here in the 14th century. The family name appears as 'atte Beche' and as 'de la Beche'.

Nearby **Haxton** means Hacun's stone. This may refer to some kind of boundary marker.

❋ FONTHILL BISHOPS, FONTHILL GIFFORD, FOVANT

The name Fonthill, first recorded as Funtgeall, in 901, is mixed Saxon and Welsh. It combines Saxon funta (water-channel) and Welsh ial (fertile uplands). For another example of ial, see Deverill. The Saxon word funta may have been borrowed from the Latin word fontana.

Fonthill Bishops shares its name with **Fonthill Gifford** and **Fonthill Brook**; it is close to **Teffont Magna**, **Teffont Evias** and near **Fovant**. All are derived from 'funta' and this concentration of funta place-names, near two Roman roads, suggests that there may have been a survival of Roman water management here and that a Latin term may have passed directly to Saxon settlers. 'Bishop' shows land was owned by the church. 'Gifford' is from Berenger Gifard who owned the manor in 1086. At Fonthill Gifford is a remarkable folly. This Gothic abbey was started in 1796 by the writer William Beckford. It was never completed and in 1825 the tower collapsed. It now survives only in part, deep within the woods. In contrast, Fovant is famous for the military badges carved into the chalk hillsides in the vicinity. They date from the First World War.

Bitham Lake at Fonthill Bishops contains the Saxon word bytme meaning bottom and refers to a place in a valley.

Stop Beacon and **Stop Farm** at Fonthill Giffard may refer to the shape

ROYAL WARWICKSHIRE

of a landscape feature if they contain a Saxon word Stoppa meaning pail, or bucket. Nearby **Greenwich Farm** contains the Saxon word wic (dairy farm).

At Fovant are **Chislebury Camp** – the fort by the shallow valley; **Touching Head Copse** meaning crossroads; **Gallows Barrow** which may refer to the site of executions.

✿ FOXLEY

Not surprisingly this is the leah (clearing) where foxes are found. This Saxon place-name was first recorded in the Domesday Book when it was known as Foxelege. **Honey Lane** probably refers to sticky, muddy ground and such references to 'honey' occur at a number of spots in Wiltshire.

✿ FROXFIELD

The spelling of this name as Forscanfeld in 803 gives little hint of its meaning. It is from two Saxon words forsc (frog) and feld (open country). A charter of 778 mentions a stream in the vicinity called Forscaburna, frog stream. This may suggest that the original meaning of the place-name was open country by the frog-stream. It was Frossefeld in 1166 and Froxefeld in 1212.

Frith Copse derives from the Saxon word fyrhthe. This can have a general meaning like wooded country, or rather more specifically of scrub on the edge of forest.

Nearby **Hugditch**, first recorded in 1385 as Hokeddych, refers to a curved ditch that once lay here. The same Saxon word 'hoc' also lies behind **Oak Hill**. The 1257 form – Hochulle – means something like hook shaped hill. However, later corruption of the name – revealed in spellings such as Okhull which appear from the 14th century – disguises the real meaning and appears to suggest some link with oak trees.

Trindledown Copse refers to the shape of the woodland and comes from the Saxon word trendel (circle).

❈ FYFIELD

This comes from the Saxon for five hides (an area of land) and in the Domesday Book there is the record of an estate of five hides being located here. Then the name was spelled Fifhide though it had become Fyfhide in 1300, Fyfilde alias Fyfitt in 1505 and Fyfelde in 1558. The chalk downland here is famous for its ancient pre-Roman field systems and for the sarsen stones of the type used to build Avebury and Stonehenge. Locally they are also called grey wethers because they resemble sheep.

•• G ••

❈ GARSDON

This name combines the two Saxon words gaers (grass) and dun (hill). First recorded in 701 as Gersdune, it has had a number of variations in its long history including Garsindun (1250) and Geersden (1675).

Church Farm may refer to land originally in Church ownership. In 1677 it was called Over Churchleys. This may suggest that at some time in its history it contained the Saxon word leah (clearing). In this case the full name would have meant the clearing owned by the Church.

🌸 GRAFTON (EAST and WEST)

The Saxon name graftun gave rise to these village names which mean settlement by the grove. The Saxon word graf seems to have had the meaning of a small, defined and possibly managed piece of woodland. In the Domesday Book it appears in the form Graftone. In the vicinity are the Grafton Disc Barrows; these two similarly sized Bronze Age burial mounds overlap and are partly overlaid by a pre-Roman field system.

Culverleaze Copse probably refers to a clearing frequented by pigeons, or doves.

Piccadilly is not unique in the county as a reference to a distant part of the parish. In these cases London is used as a measurement of distance in the same way as those places called Scotland and Ireland.

Wexcombe may mean wax valley, from bees in the area. **Wilton** probably contains the Saxon word wull (wool) and refers to a sheep farm. **Wolf Hall** was called Ulfela in the Domesday Book and takes its name from the Saxon word healh (corner of land) frequented by wolves. It may also refer to Wolf as a personal name; either derivation is possible.

🌸 GREAT WISHFORD

This village name means the ford by the wych-elm and was first recorded in the Domesday Book as Wicheford. 'Great' differentiates it from **Little Wishford** and it appeared as Muchelewychford (1332) and as Magna Wyccheford (1428).

The villagers celebrate Oak Apple Day (May 29th) by cutting wood in **Grovely Wood** and assert their right to do so with the cry 'Grovely, Grovely and all Grovely'. Recorded as Grafan lea in 940, it means ditch wood, from Saxon grafa (ditch) and leah (wood). Leah here would then be used in its older sense of a wood, rather than having its more usual meaning of a clearing. The ditch in the name is probably a reference to the Roman road (with its side ditches) which runs through the wood. The Saxon word grafa later gave rise to the modern word 'grave'; the more usual Saxon word for a ditch was dic.

Alternatively, the first element may be the Saxon word graf (grove, copse). Leah would then have its more usual meaning of a clearing. The overall meaning would then be 'clearing in a small, defined wood'. The name was Gravelinges in the Domesday Book, Grofle in 1317 and Grovelegh in 1402. It is probably the traditional activites in Grovely Wood that lie behind the curiously named **Custom Bottom**.

Dutman's Corner is a modern survival of an area called duttan hamm in an Anglo-Saxon charter and containing the word hamm (land in the bend of a river).

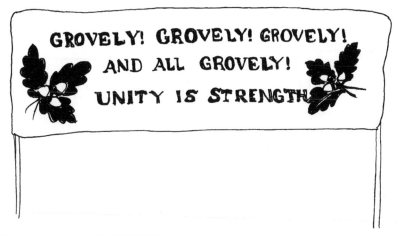

❧ GRIM'S DITCH

There are a number of prehistoric banks and dykes in Wiltshire which have this name. A number are in the vicinity of Salisbury. One marks the Wiltshire-Dorset county boundary. Grim comes from a Saxon word meaning masked, or disguised. In Saxon mythology this was an alternative name for the pagan god Woden, who was believed to sometimes travel the world in disguise. As such these names are comparable to the name of the Wansdyke (Woden's dyke). The Grim's Ditch north of Cholderton is alternatively called Devil's Ditch and represents a Christian rejection of pagan worship as the worship of the devil.

🌸 GRIMSTEAD (EAST and WEST)

Gremestede in the Domesday Book, the name means green homestead, from two Saxon words grene and hamstede. Green is probably a reference to surrounding pasture. By 1194 the spelling Grimstede was very similar to the modern form.

Butter Furlong Farm probably refers to a productive piece of land. **Gallow Hayes** was perhaps a traditional site for executions. **Redlynch Plantation** contains the Saxon word hlinc and is probably the red bank.

Nightwood Copse actually means wood belonging to the knight and this is obvious from the 14th century spelling Knyghtwode. As late as 1840 it was called Knight Wood. The Saxon word cniht meant servant, though if the name is medieval it may refer to the socially higher knight of popular imagination.

🌸 GRITTLETON

This name was first recorded in 940 as Grutelington. It means the settlement of the people living by the gravelly bank/ terraced hill. It is derived from no less than four Saxon words: greot (gravel), hlinc (bank/terraced hill), ing (the people of) and tun (settlement). It was Gritilton by 1327, though the original meaning is clear from 1687 when it was called Grittleton alias Grittlington.

The meaning of **Deadhill Wood** is obscure. In 1840 it was called simply Dead Hill but nothing more is known about its origins.

Both **Foscote** and **East Foscote** mean literally the fox cottages. The Saxon word 'cot', in these cases, was probably used as a reference to fox earths. Alternatively this could possibly contain a personal name.

Newlands Farm was Newelonde in 1279 and could refer to land newly broken in as arable. As such this is very old 'new' land indeed!

Clopton probably contains a Saxon word clop (lumpy hill), while **Grove Barn** was home to William de Grava in 1189.

·· H ··

❋ HAM

Recorded as Hamme in 931 this means land in the bend of a river, from the Saxon word hamm. It was Hame in the Domesday Book and Hama in 1166. The stream in question is a tributary of the Kennet.

Hamspray House preserves a Saxon word spraeg meaning brushwood. The name is first recorded here in 1276.

Pidgitt is an area of land derived from Pyddi's geat (gate). It was first recorded in 931 as pyddes geat.

❋ HANNINGTON

The meaning of this place-name is Hana's hill and it is formed from a Saxon personal name and the word dun. Dun is one of a group of Saxon words used to describe hills and usually one with a rounded outline. This name was first recorded in the Domesday Book as Hanindone. A more recognisable form – Hannyngton – appears in 1576.

Gore Farm is derived from the Saxon word gara, a triangular piece of land left after the furrows of an open-field system had been ploughed.

Hannington Wick would have been the wic, or dairy farm of the main village and the additional word is Saxon. In 1289 it was simply as Wyk.

Stert's Farm refers to a protruding area of land between water and comes from the Saxon word steort, which literally means tail.

❋ HARDENHUISH

Mentioned in 854 as Heregeardingc hiwisce this is the hiwisc (land sufficient for one family) belonging to Heregeard. By Domesday Book the name had contracted to Hardenehus and by 1289 Hardenehywish, which would have been pronounced very similarly to the modern form. The diarist Francis Kilvert was born in the rectory in 1840 and in the church-yard of St Nicholas is the monument to the 19th century political economist and MP, David Ricardo.

✿ HARNHAM (EAST and WEST)

In 1115 the spelling was identical to the modern form. The references to two separate settlements – East Harnham and West Harnham – first appear in the 13th century. The name probably means harahamm (land in bend of a river frequented by hares), the river being the Nadder. Harnham Hill was the site of an important early Anglo-Saxon burial ground.

Harnham Bridge was originally called pontem de Ayleswad in 1255. This is a mix of Latin and a Saxon place-name, meaning the bridge of Aegel's ford. Clearly the river was crossed here before the assistance of a bridge. The second element in Ayleswad is the Saxon word waed (a rare alternative to ford and meaning literally 'wade').

✿ HEDDINGTON

This Saxon name means Hedde's tun (settlement). It was Edintone in the Domesday Book and Hedinton in 1203.

Harley Cottages contains either the Saxon word har (old), horu (dirty), or hara (hare). The second element is leah (clearing). **Heddington Wick** is the wic (dairy farm) belonging to Heddington and was plain Wike in 1540. **Kings Play Hill** may be a reference to the Royalist victory on Roundway Down in 1643.

A striking name is **The Splatts**. It first appears in 1526 as le Splotte and is a survival of the Saxon word splot, meaning a small piece of ground.

✿ HEYTESBURY

The Domesday Book spelling of Hestrebe looks nothing like the Saxon original: Heahthryth's burg (fort). However 12th century versions (like Hehtredeberi in 1109) look more like the original. The magnificent parish church contains a chantry of the Hungerford family who made a fortune in the wool trade and had a wool store at Heytesbury. Their castle lay at Farleigh Hungerford in Somerset.

Bowls Barrow means Bodel's beorg (burial mound). The first reference to it by this name dates from 968. **Little London** is probably a humorous reference to a more distant part of the village.

Tytherington means Tiedre's tun (settlement). This is identical with two other place-names elsewhere in the county. They are **Tytherton Lucas** and **East Tytherton**.

✵ HIGHWORTH

Originally the name was just Worth from the Saxon for homestead. This is revealed in the Domesday Book name Wrde. By 1232 the element high was added as a distinguishing feature. A number of the road names are very old. **Cricklade Road** was Cryckeladys Way in 1463, **Shrivenham Road** was Shrevenham Way in 1540. The **Goldfinger** pub is named from the character in the James Bond book and film and was opened in 1972 by Ian Fleming's widow.

A local legend claims that Oliver Cromwell fired at Highworth Church from Castle Hill, near Blunsdon. However, apart from Cromwell probably not being there, 17th century field guns could not fire the three mile distance! Another local tradition asserts that Cromwell refortified one of the prehistoric earth circles known as Common Farm circles. This may be a spin-off from the previous legend.

The names **Crouch Hill** and **Little Crouch Hill** derive from a Welsh word cruc, meaning hill.

Eastrop means the east hamlet and was first recorded in the 13th century as Esthropp in Worthe. Nearby is **Westrop** which is first recorded in 1249 as Westrop and in 1302 as West Thorp juxta Heyworth.

Fresden Farm probably means in the Saxon language fersc (fresh, fine quality) dun (hill).

Hampton is first mentioned in the Domesday Book as Hantone and comes from the Saxon word haematun (village of the people). Nearby

Sevenhampton is a Saxon name and was originally the tun (settlement) of the seofonhaeme (seven homesteads).

Wicksted Farm preserves the Saxon word wic (dairy farm). The second element stede, means the place of... the site of...

�֍ HILMARTON

Called Helmerdingtun in 962, the name means the settlement of Helmheard, from two Saxon words Helmhearding and tun. By 1198 the name had shortened to Helmerton and appears as Hilmerton in 1349.

Beversbrook records the presence of an animal no longer found in Britain, the beaver; **Catcombe** does not refer to cats but to a Saxon personal name, Cada. **Clevancy** was plain Clive in the Domesday Book and is derived from the Saxon word clif (cliff/steep slope).

Corton Manor was Corfton in 1195 and contains the Saxon words corf (gap) and tun (settlement). The reference is to a landscape feature in the chalk country.

Cowage Farm is from a Saxon original cuwic (dairy farm). **Highway** was Hiwi in the Domesday Book and means the main road or the hay road.

The name **New Zealand** is not unique to this corner of Wiltshire. Such names were sometimes given to remote parts of a parish. **Witcombe** is the wide cumb (short, broad valley).

✖ HILPERTON

This is Hylpric's tun (settlement). In the Domesday Book it was spelled Helprinton. By 1268 it had become Hylperton. **Paxcroft**, now the location of a major housing development, is from the Saxon personal name Paeccel and croft (small field).

✖ HINDON

This means hill of the monks, or nuns, from the Saxon word hiwan and dun. The reference is probably to Shaftesbury Abbey. Hiwan means members of a religious community. It was spelled Hynedon in 1268 and Hindon by 1632.

Hawking Down Farm may contain a Saxon word hoc (hook) referring to a landscape feature, though it is not certain. It was Hocken Down in 1840.

❋ HINTON, BROAD

This name means the heah (high) tun (settlement). **Bincknoll Castle** derives from Saxon beonacnoll (bees' small hill). **Uffcott** was Ufecote in the Domesday Book and means Uffa's cottage.

❋ HINTON, LITTLE

This probably means the settlement belonging to the religious community, from the Saxon words hiwan and tun. **Earl's Court Farm** was Ardescote in the Domesday Book and has nothing to do with earls. It means the cottage of a Saxon with a name starting with Eard.

❋ HOLT

The name was spelled in 1242 as now and means the wood, from a Saxon word holt. Research suggests this word was often used of single-species woodland. **The Ham Tree** pub takes its name from such a tree which once stood opposite, on **Ham Green**. The area known as **The Midlands** probably derives from its fairly central place within the linear settlement. **Gaston**, close to Holt, is derived from the Saxon gaers (grass) tun (settlement). **Oxen Leaze Farm** contains the Saxon word laes (pasture).

The **Star** appears to derive from a field-name, which itself may have its source in the Saxon word staefer (stakes) referring to a fenced enclosure.

❋ HORNINGSHAM

Only the presence of the letter 's' differentiates the modern appearance of this name from the Domesday Book version, Horningham. The name means settlement of the people of the place called Horn, from OE Horning and ham. In Wiltshire 'ham' is quite rare and 'tun' is more usual. The name of **Baycliff Farm** was first recorded in the Domesday Book. It is Saxon and means Baegloc's clif (steep hillside).

❧ HUISH

Called Iwis in the Domesday Book, it simply means the household, from a Saxon word hiwisc. It probably referred to land large enough to maintain one small family. It was later variously spelled Hiwis (1162), Hywych (1279), Hewishe (1629).

A legend claims that a ghostly cortege has been seen on the nearby Wansdyke. According to this the cortege consisted of a coffin on a wagon drawn by black horses. A golden crown sat on the coffin and the cortege was escorted by men carrying flaming torches.

❧ HULLAVINGTON

The Domesday Book spelling of Hunlavintone indicates the settlement of Hunlaf, from the Saxon Hunlafingtun. The present spelling first appears in 1583. The church of St Mary's contains a finely embroidered priest's cope, worked in silver and gold.

Bradfield Farm is from a Saxon original bradfeld (wide open land). **Furleaze Farm** is the further, or remote laes (pasture).

Piccadilly is one of a number in Wiltshire and refers to a place at the edge of the village. It uses London as a measurement of remoteness. **Stock Wood** contains the Saxon word stocc (stump).

Townleaze Barn comes from a Saxon original tunlaes and means the settlement with pasture. In this case as in a large number of examples tun is used of the smallest of settlements and means 'farm'.

Nearby **Surrendell** is probably derived from a Saxon name like surandene (sour large valley). Why it attracted such a name is not known.

·· I ··

❋ IDMISTON

First recorded in 947 as Idemestone the name means Idmaer's tun (settlement).

Birdlime Farm is a fascinating example of how a name whose meaning is no longer apparent owing to linguistic changes can be corrupted out of all recognition. A chapel was founded here in the early 14th century by Lucia Burgelon. However by 1554 the name had been corrupted to Burdlyme and from here it developed to its quite misleading modern form.

Gomeldon. This is from the Saxon personal name Gumela and dun (hill). The earliest spelling was Gomeledona in 1189. There was another place nearby called Gomelhamdoun in 1321. This suggests a place-name Gumela's ham (village) as well as Gumela's hill.

Hale Farm is actually an abbreviation of Halfurlong recorded in 1518. **Porton** means the tun (settlement) by a river with a name something like Power. It appears in the Domesday Book as Portone and in 1312 as Pourton juxta Gomeledon.

❋ IFORD

Perched on the border with Somerset Iford is derived from the Saxon iegford, meaning island ford. The name first appears in 987 as Igford. The element ieg is the West Saxon dialect form of 'eg' (island). There is no island here – the reference is probably to dry ground above the marshy valley of the River Frome. It is now famous for Iford Manor, with its terraced gardens. A statue of Britannia commands the bridge over the river. Local tradition has it that the statue once faced downstream but was turned about to its present position because Britannia should face the waves.

❋ IMBER

The modern name looks very different to that recorded in the Domesday

Book – Imemerie. However, this earlier version is closer to its original meaning of Imma's pond, from the Saxon name Imma and mere (pond). The name had shortened to Imere by 1291 and appears as Immer alias Imber in 1540. In southern counties mere can refer to a small pool or pond, rather than a lake.

Imma's name also appears in the lost names Ymmanedene (Imma's dun, or hill) in nearby Eddington parish and Imendone (same meaning) in Imber parish. Imber itself was taken over by the military in World War Two and is no longer inhabited.

❋ INGLESHAM

Recorded as Inggeneshamm (950) and Inglesham (1160), this name means Ingin's land in the bend of a river, from the Saxon name Ingin and hamm. The rivers here are the Thames and the Cole. Inglesham church contains a fine statue of the Virgin and infant Christ. It is an example of 11th century West Saxon craftsmanship. The Virgin sits in a chair with Christ on her lap holding a book. Over the child's head the hand of God points towards His son. Above the Virgin's head are carved the letters 'Maria'. Below her a sundial is carved, suggesting that originally the stone was built into the southern wall of the church. The church – of St John the Baptist – is a small 13th century building containing 14th century screens, and 17th century pews, pulpit and reading desk. In addition there are wall paintings. The nave of the church may well be a late Saxon construction.

Lynt Bridge. The name of this bridge is taken from an older name for what is now the river Cole. **Upper Inglesham** was first recorded in 1279 in the form Overenglesham.

•• K ••

❋ KEEVIL

This village, with its fine collection of old houses, takes its name from the Saxon Cyfaleah (Cyfa's clearing). A charter of 964 gives the spelling as

Kefle. In Domesday Book the appearance was very different, being Chivele. It was not until 1318 that the spelling – Keyvele – approached the present pronunciation.

Baldham Bridge takes its name from an otherwise unknown Saxon landowner, Bealda, and the word hamm (land in the bend of a river). **Keevil Wick** adds the Saxon word wic (dairy farm) to the name of the village. The sense is that this would have been a secondary settlement belonging to Keevil. It was first recorded in 1279 as Kyvele Wyk.

Both **Longleaze Farm** and **Oxen Leaze Farm** contain the Saxon word laes, meaning pasture. In each case the pasture was identified by a particular characteristic, long in the former and used by oxen in the latter. The pasture that gave rise to Oxen Leaze Farm was called Oxenlese in 1327.

Mere Farm takes its name from a Saxon word for lake or pond. In southern England the meaning can be a very small body of water.

Pantry Bridge has nothing to do with kitchens but takes its name from the Saxon pintreow (pine-tree bridge). This is an interesting example of the way in which spellings of place-names are sometimes corrupted over time in order to make sense of them. This can end with them looking nothing like their original spelling and with their meaning obscured.

KELLAWAYS

Originally this was Tuderyngton Kaylewey and took its name from Tytherton near Chippenham (as it was a manor of this estate) and a landowning family, the de Cailleweys, or de Kailleweys. Eventually the first part was dropped leaving only the name of the family, which became that of the village. The modern **Kellaways Bridge** was Caisway in about 1540 when it probably took its name from Maud Heath's Causeway, the routeway which was built to enable travellers to cross the flooded Avon valley to market at Chippenham (see **Chippenham**). However by 1584 it had become Kelloways bridge and this name has stuck. At Kellaways the causeway – which runs for 4½ miles through the Avon valley – is raised about 1.8m above modern road level and carried on 60 raised arches. At one point on the line of the causeway an inscribed sundial marks the route. The causeway was later crossed by a railway line and a pass under the line was constructed.

At the top of Wick Hill there is a monument to Maud, the traditional builder of the causeway. The monument was erected in 1838 and paid for by William Lisle Bowles, the parson of Bremhill, and by the Marquis of Lansdowne. There is another inscribed stone where the causeway ends in Chippenham.

❧ KEMBLE

Recorded as Kemele in 682, this name did not approach its present spelling until 1523 when it appears as Kembyll. It probably means the border, from the Welsh word 'cyfyl', derived from the earlier British 'komel'.

Nearby **Ewen** is derived from the Saxon word awielm, meaning source of a river. The spring in question is the one now called **Thames Head**. This is apparent as the field it rises in is called Yeowing, a word clearly related to Ewing.

Kemble Wick was plain Weeke in 1591 and means the wic (dairy farm) belonging to Kemble. The word is Saxon.

❧ KENNET (EAST and WEST)

East Kennet was first called Estkenette in 1267; the earliest reference was simply to Cynetan in an Anglo-Saxon charter of 939. The place-name is from the river Kennet, derived from the British Cunetio; ancestor of the Welsh language. It may be from an ancient Celtic word cuno (dog), or from some hillfort with a name like cuno (high). Either way the evidence is inconclusive. There was an Iron Age tribe in Spain with the name Cunetes but this throws little light on what must remain a mystery.

East Kennet long barrow dates from the New Stone Age and is a great tree-covered mound about 105m long and 6m tall. There is evidence that it once had side ditches and would have been a communal burial mound like the more famous excavated example at nearby West Kennet.

Langdean is from the Saxon for long denu (large valley). In 1289 it was referred to as Langedeneswyk, implying that there was a wic (dairy) farm here which took its name from that of the valley. For West Kennet see **Avebury**.

❧ KILMINGTON

The settlement of Cynehelm, from Saxon Cynehelmingtun. It was Cileme-tone in Domesday Book, Culminton in 1251 and Kylmyngton alias Cul-myngton in 1403.

Norton Farm derives from the Saxon for north tun (settlement). It is north of Stourton, and is recorded in the Domesday Book as Nortone.

White Sheet Hill probably means the white slope and the word 'sheet' may be related to a German word sciez (steep place). This would suggest there was a similar Saxon word. In the 17th century it had the alternative name of Beacon Hill and so it is unknown exactly when it acquired its present name. On top of the hill is an enclosure dating from the New Stone Age. It encloses about 1.6ha and the earth bank is crossed by 21 causeways. The enclosure was probably a communal seasonal meeting place. When it was excavated in 1951 the ditch was found to be about 3m wide and from 0.3 to 1.5m deep. On the bottom fragments of pottery and the skull of an ox were discovered. In the Bronze Age, on the east side of the camp later generations erected a bowl barrow; when this was excavated in 1807 a skeleton was unearthed.

❧ KINGTON LANGLEY

This is the long leah (clearing) belonging to Kington St Michael. In the Domesday Book it was plain Langhelei; in 1289 it had become North-langele; in 1636 it was Langley Kington.

California Cottages are so named because they are at the edge of the parish. The same reasoning may explain **South Sea Farm**. **Morrell Cottages** are derived from the Saxon gemaerewiell (boundary spring).

Fitzurse Farm is an interesting survival of the name of Urso who held land at Langhelie at the time of the compilation of the Domesday Book. At various times it has had the alternative names of Nether Langley and Langley Fitzurs (both in the 16th century).

🦋 KINGTON ST MICHAEL

Recorded as Kingtone, in 934, this name means either king's settlement, from Saxon cyning and tun, or royal settlement, if the first element was Saxon cyne. The church dedication is also included in the name.

Bulidge House contains a Saxon place-name meaning bull hide. The word hide refers to an area of land and the meaning may suggest a piece of land where a bull was kept. It was Bolhides in the early 17th century.

Cromhall Farm has its roots in the Saxon words crumb (bent) healh (corner) and may refer to a landscape feature. **Heywood Farm** contains the Saxon word for hedge and indicates a wood bounded by some form of enclosure.

Moorshall Farm was morsceagan in 1043 and joins two Saxon words, mor (wild, marshy land) and sceaga (small wood). The word sceaga was also used of underwood forming the edge of a field. By 1279 the name had developed into la Morshawe and by 1517 a very recognisable Moreshall. **Priory Farm** takes its name from a priory of Benedictine nuns once located here.

Tor Hill probably contains the Welsh word tor (high place) found at a number of West Country locations (eg Glastonbury Tor).

🦋 KINGTON, WEST

First known as Westkinton, in 1194, it means the same as the last name. It is 5 miles due west of Kington St Michael, within two miles of which, to the east, is Kington Langley. These names are survivals of a significant royal estate in the area.

Harcombe Wood is the har (old) cumb (short, broad valley). There is some suggestion that the Saxon word har was used to indicate boundaries, in the sense 'an old established point'. This may apply here as it is on the parish boundary and many such boundaries date from before the Norman Conquest.

Maggs Grove Farm was Maggs Grave in 1840. However it is difficult to tell which is the original meaning and which the corruption.

KNOOK

Although the Domesday Book spelling – Cunuche – is very different to the modern one, the pronunciation of the second syllable of the 11th century name was similar. It means hillock, from the Welsh word cnwc. By 1211 it had developed into Cnuke, by 1227 Knuke and in 1581 it was Knooke. It is now home to the army's Knook Camp, separated from the village itself by the A36.

The Domesday Book tells us that in 1086 the manor here was owned by a woman, Leofgyth, who made gold-thread embroidery for the king and queen. A fine carving in Knook church shows a lion and a griffin biting the trunk of a tree while being held in the branches. This carving probably dates from the 10th or 11th century.

Ansty Hill was Anstrow Hill in 1773 and is probably derived from two Saxon words: anstig (narrow path) and treow (tree), the sense being a narrow path by some trees.

KNOYLE (EAST and WEST)

Recorded as Cnugel in 948, it means knuckle shaped hill, from the Saxon word cnugel. This word is not actually recorded before the Norman Conquest but it existed in Middle English as 'knokel' and was clearly derived from a Saxon original. By 1200 the name was recorded in the more familiar form Knoel. In 1408 it was Knoyell.

East Knoyle first appears in this form in 1467 (Esteknoyle). While this is the version of the name that survived it had a number of other names in its long history. At various times it was called Childecnowell (1204), Knowel Magna (1285), Knowell Episcopi (1346), Estknoyle alias Bisshopes Knoyle (1570). The reference to 'child' may in fact mean young retainers rather than children. Bishop refers to the fact that the Bishop of Winchester owned land here.

Coleman's Farm, **Friar's Hayes** and **King's Bushes** all derive from local landholders. The first two were 16th and 17th century respectively; the last one 14th century. **Milton** is nothing to do with mills. The 1281 spelling – Middelton – shows it comes from the Saxon for middle settlement. **Pertwood** probably derives from the Welsh word perta (copse).

Sheephouse Farm has carried this name since at least 1570 when it was Shepehowse. **Summerleaze Farm** refers to the laes (pasture) used in the summer. **Vernhill** is actually fern hill and an interesting example of the way in which an 'f' can change to a 'v' in Wiltshire dialect. **Windmill Hill** has been so called since at least 1632.

West Knoyle was first called this in 1467 (Westeknoyle). Like East Knoyle it too has had alternative names, including Knoel Parva (1428), Knoel Hodyerne (1428), Little Knoyell (1408). The name Hodyerne comes from Hodierna the foster-mother of Richard the Lionheart, who owned land here in the 12th century. **Broadmead Farm** means the large meadow. The same kind of attempt to define the appearance of land lies behind **Longmead Coppice**. **Oxleaze Farm** is the laes (pasture) used by oxen. **Puckwell** refers to local superstitions as it contains a Saxon word which continued into the medieval period and into modern times as a word for a goblin. Clearly local legend claimed that a goblin lived in the well. **Wood Farm** was bosco de Knoel in 1279, a Latin form of the name.

❧ LACOCK

The modern name of this lovely stone-built village is little different from the earliest spelling, Lacok in a Saxon charter of 854. It means little stream, from the Saxon word lacuc, related to 'lacu' (little stream). Lacock Abbey – now a National Trust property and home to the Fox Talbot Museum of Photography – was originally an abbey founded in the 13th century by Ella, Countess of Salisbury.

Abbey Farm unsurprisingly refers to the monastic house at Lacock. **Bewley** was recorded as Beulee in 1257 and means the leah (clearing) where beaw (gadfly) can be found.

Bowden is Saxon for above the down and would originally have been bufandune. In the 13th century it was Bovedone and the meaning is clear. In 1561 it was Bovedon alias Bowdon and it is a variant of the latter name that has stuck. The area called **Inwood** refers to woodland directly man-

Lacock

aged from the home-farm of the abbey estate. In 1289 it was called bosco de Lacok (Latin for 'wood of Lacock').

Lackham, now the home of the agricultural college, means the hamm (land in the bend of a river) belonging to Lacock. It was called Lacham in the Domesday Book.

Nash Hill was le Hasshe in 1270 and means 'at the ash tree'. The present form of the name obscures the meaning but it is very clear from the 1304 spelling which is in the form le Asshe.

Nethercote is the lower cot (cottage) and the name is Saxon, though is first recorded in 1337. **Notton** was Natton in 1232 and Netton in 1284. It means cattle settlement from two Saxon words neat (cattle) and tun.

Reybridge looks quite different to the form Ebrigge which appeared in the late 13th century. This spelling shows that the meaning lies in a Saxon eabrycg, which means literally water-bridge. The spelling with 'r' first appears in 1513, in the form Raybrigge, and quite obscures the original meaning.

Wick Farm is one of a large number of minor names in Wiltshire formed from the Saxon word wic, meaning dairy farm. In 1232 it was plain Wyke, though in 1289 its location was clarified in the form Lacokeswyk. An alternative name – Cherlaweswyke – appeared in 1316 and this lingered locally as a variation on it – Charles Week – was recorded in the mid 18th century. The meaning of this variant of the name is obscure and it did not ultimately survive.

LANDFORD

Recorded as Langeford in the Domesday Book, the name is derived from the Saxon lanuford (ford on the lane). The meaning is clear in the 1242 form, Laneford. The intruding 'd' first appears in 1295 in the form Landeford.

Nearby **Earldoms Farm** takes its name from the Earl of Pembroke, the owner of the land. **Pugpits Copse** comes from the Saxon word puca (goblin). It is clearly a reference to a local superstition.

The Slings is so called because it is a thin piece of woodland and was obviously reminiscent of the leather thong of a sling. **Witterns Hill Farm** takes its name from Richard Whytehorne, a landowner in 1348.

LANGFORD (HANGING and STEEPLE)

In 943 the name Langanforda probably referred to both settlements. The name means long ford, from Saxon lang and ford. **Hanging Langford** is first recorded in 1242 and means a sloping site. **Steeple Langford** is first recorded in 1291 and refers to the church steeple. In 1435 one of the Langfords was named Tokynglangford, after its fulling (tucking) mill, but the name did not survive.

Bathampton means the bathing place belonging to the village of the people. In the Domesday Book it was Bachentune, though a more revealing Bethampton is found in a record of 1222. The evidence suggests that in its long history the place has been variously called Batham and Bathampton. Though slightly different, the meaning is substantially similar for both forms of the name.

The Spectacles is a curious name for an area of woodland and was probably inspired by the shape of the wood.

Yarnbury Castle was earnaburg in Saxon and means the fort of the eagles. It was first mentioned in 1591 and then called Yarneberrie castell.

❀ LANGLEY BURRELL

The meaning of the name – long clearing, from Saxon langleah – is apparent in the earliest spelling of the name, Langelegh in 940. By 1289 it had developed into Langleye, very similar to the modern form. Burrell is from Petrus Burel, who owned the manor in 1242.
The way in which place-names can be subtly corrupted by their similarity to another name is clearly seen in the name of **Barrow Farm**. At first glance it would appear to take its name from the Saxon word beorg (hill, or burial mound) and this would be a reasonable inference. However, a spelling dating from 1227 shows that then it was Barwe and this indicates that in fact it is derived from another Saxon word, in this case bearu (grove). However, without an early record the meaning would be obscured by later changes to the name. It is a salutary warning to place-name students to be on their guard!

Birds Marsh was recorded as Birch Marsh in 1840 and takes its name from trees rather than from birds. **Cocklebury**, first recorded in 1181 as Kokelesberga, may take its name either from seashells apparent as fossils in local rocks, or from the plant corn-cockle.

❀ LATTON

This is either the leactun (settlement where vegetables grow), or the lacutun (settlement beside the stream). It was Latone to the compilers of the Domesday Book and in 1249 was Latteton.

Nearby **Eisey** contains the Saxon word ieg (island, well drained land in a marsh) though the first element is obscure. It was Esig in a charter of 775 and Aisi in the Domesday Book.

Water Eaton was Etone in the Domesday Book, Nunyeton in 1281, Eton Monial in 1332, Waterheton in 1395 and West Eaton alias Water Yetton in

1726. All in all a remarkable collection of aliases! The name is Saxon for settlement by a river and derives from two words ea (water) and tun (settlement). The reference to nuns in 1281 was due to ownership of the manor by the nuns of Godstow.

❧ LAVERSTOCK

Recorded as Lawrecestohes in the Domesday Book, it means outlying farm frequented by larks, from Saxon laewerc and stoc. Stoc is often used for subsidiary settlements.

Ford once had the much longer name of Winterburneford, recorded in 1189. Not surprisingly it is the site of a ford over the river Bourne, which was once called the Winterbourne.

Milford was Meleford in the Domesday Book and means the ford by the mill. It was called Mulleford Richard in 1354, after a landowner, but though such surnaming of a place is common it did not stick in this case.

Something of a mystery surrounds the name of **St Thomas's Bridge**. Why it was called this is not clear. In 1540 it was Thomas Beketes Bridge, which clearly links it to the 12th century Archbishop of Canterbury.

❧ LAVINGTON (MARKET and WEST)

The Saxon original name of both these villages was Lafingtun, meaning the settlement of Lafa, or Lafa's people. In the Domesday Book the spelling was Laventone, which had developed into Lavintone by 1091. **West Lavington** is also known as Bishop's Lavington because it was a manor of the diocese of Salisbury.

Market Lavington was called Chepynglavynton in 1397, the first element derived from the Saxon word for market. It was also known as Steeple Lavington and this form first appears in 1242 but did not survive.

Market Lavington has a number of interesting names close by. **Black Dog Farm** takes its name from a public house. **Fiddington** is derived from the Saxon word for a settlement of five hides. This was an area of land capable of supporting a Saxon thegn, a warrior nobleman. **Frieth**

Farm comes from the Saxon fyrhthe (wooded country). **Gibbet Knoll** probably indicates the site of public executions.

West Lavington too has interesting names in its vicinity. **Littleton Pannell** was plain Liteltone (small settlement) in the Domesday Book, though by 1317 it had taken the form Lutleton Paynel after a 13th century landowner. **Rams Cliff** does not actually refer to sheep but rather to ravens and this is revealed in the spelling Remesclive dating from 1227, suggesting an origin in the Saxon word hremnes (ravens).

❧ LEA

This simply means the clearing from the Saxon word leah. In 1190 the name was recorded as Lia. In 1346 it was la Lee juxta Malmesbury.

Nearby **Cleverton** was Claverdon in the 13th century. It derives from a Saxon original, claefredun (rounded hill where clover grows).

Crabb Mill may contain a reference to crab-apple trees but it is difficult to tell as the earliest record dates back only to 1632.

Cross Farm may take its name from Christian services conducted during the medieval perambulations of the parish. **Winkworth** is Wineca's worth (homestead). It appeared in 1193 as Winekeswurda.

❧ LEIGH

This name means simply the clearing and is from the common Saxon word leah. In 1242 it was called Lia, though it has had a variety of names: Legh juxta Ashton (1289), Legh juxta Crekelade (1368), Lye alias Ligh alias Leigh (1699).

Cove Farm contains the Saxon word cofa, in this case some form of shelter. **Knapp Farm** derives from the Saxon word cnaepp, meaning small hill.

Waterhay is nothing to do with hay but rather contains the Saxon word gehaeg (hedge). The sense is probably 'the hedge by the water'. **White Spire** has carried this name since the middle of the 17th century and the reference is probably to tall trees as it was a wood name in 1650.

❧ LEIGH DELAMERE

Now more famous as a service station on the M4 motorway, the name first appeared in 1236 as Leye, becoming Lye Dallamer in the 16th century. In its history it has also been called Lye juxta Lokyngton (1412) and Legh juxta Castelcomb (1534). The name is from the Saxon leah (clearing) to which has been added the name of Adam de la Mare who owned the land here in 1236.

Green Barrow Farm refers to a burial mound, or barrow, found in the vicinity of the farm.

Sevington means the settlement made up of seven homes. The original would have been formed from three Saxon words, seofon, haeme and tun. In 1043 the place was called Seofonhaemtune. By 1512 it had shortened to Seyvyngton.

❧ LIDDINGTON

Called Lidentune in a charter of 940, a more familiar spelling appears in 1205 in the form Lidinton, though in 1636 it was called Luddington. It means settlement on the river Hlyde, from the Saxon river name Hlyde and tun (settlement).

The second part of **Liddington Wick** is derived from Saxon wic (dairy farm).

Nearby **Liddington Castle** was probably originally called Badbury, though this name has now been transferred to a neighbouring village (see **Badbury**).

Medbourne is the meadow burna (stream). Saxon burna was a word used for clear streams in chalk country.

❧ LIMPLEY STOKE

Originally this was Hangyndestok (in 1263) and meant the hanging outlying farm, from the Saxon words hangian and stoc (outlying farm). The name clearly referred to the steep river-cliff of the Avon here. In 1585 its name was recorded as Lympley Stoke. The meaning of the first word is unclear: the first element may be a Saxon personal name but it is not certain; the second element is the Saxon word leah (clearing).

Ashleigh was Ashley in 1642 and means the ash-tree leah (clearing). **Winyatts** is the wind gap and refers to an exposed place.

❧ LITTLETON DREW

The name, first recorded in 1065 as Litletun, comes from the Saxon for little settlement. Drew is from a medieval Norman-French landowner. Littleton Dru first makes its appearance in 1311.

West Dunley was Dynelawe in 1289 and possibly means the hlaew (burial mound) on the dun (hill) but the first element is uncertain. **Gatcombe Hill** is from the Saxon name gatacumb (goats' valley). Cumb was usually applied to relatively short, broad valleys.

The Gib, called Gibraltar in 1830, is at the extreme south of the parish and was probably named to suggest its distance from the village. **Old-lands** may refer to an area of land with a long established history of cultivation, or management. It has been called this since at least 1513.

The **Salutation** inn probably originally referred to the Annunciation when the Angel Gabriel visited the Virgin Mary.

❧ LONGLEAT

Now the site of the stately home of Lord Bath the name was first recorded as Langelete in 1235. It means long watercourse, derived from the Saxon words lang and gelaet. The word gelaet, or laet, was used of artificial channels. A slightly more familiar spelling appears in 1245 as Longalete; though in 1297 the form La Longe Lete appears more French than English, as is not uncommon in the 13th century. The stately home was built in 1567-79 for the Thynne family, on the site of an earlier house built in 1550 but largely destroyed by fire. It occupied the site of a 13th century Augustinian priory.

❋ LUCKINGTON

This is Luca's settlement and is a Saxon name. It was Lochintone in the Domesday Book, Luchinton in 1198 and Lookington in 1585. **Cherry Orchard Lane** takes its name from Cherry Orchard House. **Luckley** is Luca's leah (clearing) and is clearly a reference to the same Anglo-Saxon landowner recorded in Luckington's name.

Lyppiatt Barn takes its name from the Saxon word hlypgeat (leap gate), which describes a barrier to contain sheep but which can be leaped by deer. **Wick Farm** contains the Saxon word which means a dairy farm and is found in a large number of minor names in Wiltshire.

Giants Cave reveals a local tradition of a giant asleep in a burial mound. This is a common legend and occurs at a number of sites in Wiltshire. In this case the word 'grave' has been corrupted to 'cave'. That this has happened is apparent because in 1840 the name was recorded as Giants Grave. However, the idea of a cave was present even then as nearby a Cave Tump was recorded. This clearly referred to a local belief that a burial mound was hollow. Over time the two names have been combined to give the present one. The actual reference is to a New Stone Age long barrow, which was excavated in 1646 and found to contain five or six chambers.

❋ LUDGERSHALL

This is a very interesting name. In 1015 it was recorded as Lutegaresheale, as Ludkereshala in 1150 and by 1422 a more familiar Ludgarshale. It may mean Lutegar's hollow grazing ground, from a Saxon word, gaershealh. The second element (a West Saxon form of halh, or hollow) may also mean a detached grassy area, or one surrounded by water, or marsh. There is a possibility that the whole name denotes hollow of the trapping spear (some kind of hunting trap) as lutegar could be trap-spear. **Winchester Street** goes back to at least 1515, when the market area was called le Shamelles (meaning butchers' stalls).

Shoulder of Mutton Copse is one of a number of areas of woodland carrying this name in Wiltshire. The name refers to the shape of the wood.

❧ LYDIARD (MILLICENT and TREGOZE)

In 901 the name was spelled Lidgerd. The second element of the name is the Welsh word garth (hill) but it is not clear what the first element means. By the time of the Domesday Book the name was being spelled Lidiarde. The two separate settlements first appear in the Middle Ages. In the forms Lidgard Milisent and Lidgard Tregos they appear in 1257. Millicent is from a 12th century female landowner. Tregoze is from Robert Traigoz who owned land here in 1242.

In the vicinity of **Lydiard Millicent** are a number of interesting place-names. **The Butts** refer to medieval archery practice. **Parley Copse** was called le Purlye in 1611 and means the pear tree leah (clearing). **Shaw** was called Shaghe in 1332 and takes its name from the Saxon word sceaga (copse, possibly underwood border of a field). **Sparcell's Farm** is first recorded in 1263 as Speresholt and derives from two Saxon words, spere (spear) and holt (wood, often with one predominant species). It may mean that the wood was used for hunting, or supplied the wood for spear-shafts.

Lydiard Tregoze also has some interesting place-names nearby. **Frith Copse** contains the Saxon word fyrhthe (wooded country, land overgrown with scrub). **Mannington** is the hill belonging to Mehha. Despite the superficial resemblance of the last element to the Saxon word tun (settlement), the spelling preserved in 900 – Mehandun – shows that it actually comes from dun (hill). **Midgehall** was micghaema in 983 and means in Saxon, healh (corner of land) where midges are found. **Wick Farm** contains the Saxon word wic (dairy farm). The same word is found in **Wickfield** which probably means the wic in/by the feld (open country).

❧ LYNEHAM

This is derived from Saxon linhamm (land in the bend of a river where flax is grown). The second element in this case may mean promontory of dry land in a marshy area. It is now beside a large RAF base and this is reflected in street names such as **Comet Close** and **Lancaster Square**, inspired by aircraft names. Other street names such as **Mallard Avenue** and **Pintail Court** reveal the frequent modern habit of theme naming, in this case of flying creatures rather than machines.

The last part of nearby **Bradenstoke-cum-Clack** contains a Swedish word klack (hill). It is doubtful that the word came direct from Sweden and there may have been a similar Saxon word, now lost. Bradenstoke is a Saxon name and means stoc (outlying settlement) belonging to Braydon Forest.

Preston was the priest's tun (settlement) and must have been land belonging to the Church.

Shaw Farm is derived from the Saxon word sceage (copse, or underwood at the edge of a field).

·· M ··

❀ MADDINGTON

This means the tun (settlement) of the maidens and was first recorded in 1198 as Medinton. Earlier it had been called Wintreburne (Domesday Book) and Maydenwintreburne (1270). The maidens were the nuns of Amesbury who owned land here.

Addeston means the tun (settlement) of the abbot and this is clear from 1279 when it was Abboteston. Earlier, as with Maddington, it had been called Wintreburne, a name which covered a number of settlements at the time of the writing of the Domesday Book in 1086.

Bourton Farm takes its name from a Saxon original burgtun, meaning the defended settlement. The place was first recorded in 1327 as Bourton(e). **Homanton Farm** was called Hughemanton in the 13th century, Hugmanton in 1268 and Wynterborn Homanton in 1375. It means the tun (settlement) of the hukman (small trader). It seems likely that the name was given after the Norman Conquest and this is another example of the way in which the Saxon place-name forming element 'tun' continued to be used for some time after 1066.

Oram's Grave is from a suicide buried at the crossroads here in 1849. Suicides were traditionally not buried in consecrated ground but at crossroads.

MALMESBURY

In 731 the Saxon historian Bede referred to the place as Maildufi urbs. This was a Latinised form of a probable Saxon name Maildufesburg, meaning the fort of Maeldub. In 770 the Saxon churchman Boniface referred to the place as Maldubia civitate (the second word being the Latin for town). Later versions of the name include Maldmesbyrig in 1050 and Malmesberie in the Domesday Book. According to very old traditions Maeldub was an Irish holy man who came to the West Country in about 640. He came to a land only recently converted from paganism and set up a monastery at Malmesbury. One of his pupils was the Saxon St Aldhelm. Later the West Saxon King Athelstan was buried here. The modern name of the town may be due to a confusion between the names of Maeldub and Aldhelm.

Ancient street-names include **Burnivale** from Saxon burnfeall (river fall) meaning a weir; **Cross Hayes** (recorded as Croshayes in 1300) refers to the market cross; **The Horsefair** has been called this since at least 1670. One street-name of 1603, now lost, clearly referred to a blind alley with the charming name Turne againe lane. **Westport**, now absorbed into the town, was originally a separate settlement and its name meant the place west of the town. In this case the word port meant a market-town.

Nearby **Angrove Farm** means the grove by the river Avon and was called Angrave in about 1300. In 1547 it was confusingly called Anne Grove, which was obviously an attempt to – wrongly – make sense of a place-name which no longer communicated its meaning owing to linguistic changes.

A similar attempt to make sense of a name may lie behind **Back Bridge**. It actually derives from the Saxon for Bacga's bridge and was Baggebrugge in the 13th century.

Burton Hill is the burg (fort) tun (settlement) in Saxon and the fort is probably Malmesbury itself. The sense is therefore the settlement near Malmesbury.

Cole Park derives from cufalod, the Saxon name for a cow fold. In 1065 it was Cusfalde. The meaning is very clear in the form Cowfold recorded in 1535. This had altered to Colepark in 1637 though some memory of its original meaning lingered as in 1727 it was called Cole Park alias Cowfield Park.

Malmesbury Abbey

Corston was Corstuna in 1065 and means tun (settlement) on the cors (boggy stream). Its closeness to Malmesbury helps explain its name – Corston juxta Malmesbury – recorded in 1302.

Filands takes its name from the Saxon word fielging (newly broken-in land).

Hyam was Hyham in 1300 and comes from two Saxon words, heah (high) and hamm (land in the bend of a river). The second element could be ham (village) but this element is not common in Wiltshire and the topography makes the first derivation more likely. The river in question is the Avon.

Kingway has a modern appearance but it is in fact an ancient name. In a charter of 931 it was Kingweye and looked remarkably like its modern spelling. It takes its name from the king's highway from Malmesbury to Chippenham.

Milbourne means the mill stream and was Melburne in 1249. In 1394 it was Nuthermulburne, in which the first element is the Saxon word neothera (lower).

Rodbourne is derived from reed burna (stream).

✳ MANNINGFORD (ABBOTS, BOHUN and BRUCE)

This is the ford of Manna's people, from a Saxon original Manningaford. **Abbots** is from the Abbey of St Peter at Winchester, **Bohun** is from Henry de Boun who owned the manor in 1212, **Bruce** is from Briouze in Normandy. The name was Maningaford in 987, which shows it to be derived from 'ingatun' ('the settlement of the people of...'). Most Wiltshire examples of this type of name are derived from the singular 'ingtun' and refer to an individual, not to a group named from their leader.

Swanborough Tump at **Manningford Abbots** means the burial mound of the peasants and probably referred to a settlement of estate workers in the vicinity. **The Butts** is a reference to medieval archery.

Bottlesford near **Manningford Bohun** is not derived from bottles but rather from Botwell's ford and in 1348 was Bottewelleford.

Frith Wood near **Manningford Bruce** takes its name from the Saxon word fyrhthe (wooded country, land overgrown with scrub). The church of St Peter at Manningford Bruce is a complete 12th century building.

✳ MARDEN

Recorded as Mercdene in 941 and Meresdene in the Domesday Book the name means boundary in the large valley, derived from the Saxon words gemaere/mearc (boundary) and denu (large valley). By 1242 it had reached a form – Merden – similar to the modern spelling. The little village stands inside the largest henge monument found in Britain. This is an earthwork bank and ditch which, with the south and west sides formed by the river Avon, surrounds the village. In 1969 excavations revealed the ditch was at least 15m wide but only 1.8m deep. As with other such henges it was not a defensive structure but a New Stone Age communal gathering place. Just inside the entrance was a timber building revealed through excavation as a timber circle and three post holes to support a roof. Ancient visitors to the site deposited pottery, antler picks, flint tools and animal bones in the ditch.

The site of **Hatfield Barrow** is supposed to be the burial place of a great treasure. Unfortunately this huge barrow, reputedly once about 13m high, was excavated in 1807 but no grave was found and the site was later levelled. Another local tradition was that the barrow was the burial place of men killed in battle. Another legend claims that a battle took place on the downs by Marden between men with red heads and men with black heads. The tradition claims that those with red heads won and the dead were buried in a cave. The 'cave' is very possibly a reference to Hatfield Barrow.

MARLBOROUGH

This handsome town was recorded as Merleberge in the Domesday Book. Later versions of the name include Marborowe in 1485 and Marlebroughe in 1596. The name probably means Maerla's burial mound, or hill, from the Saxon name Maerla and beorg, which can mean both tumulus and hill. It is possible that the Saxon word for the chalkland autumn gentian plant – 'meargealla' – may provide the first element. In 1215 Alexander Neckham, later abbot of Cirencester, claimed it meant Merlin's burial mound. This was inspired by the Arthurian legends and without foundation. The prehistoric mound in the town is still called Merlin's Mount. It is the second largest barrow in England, surpassed only by nearby Silbury Hill. It stands almost 100m in diameter and is 18m tall. In 1650 it was reshaped with a path spiralling round it.

Street-names in Marlborough include **Barn Street**, actually derived from Baronestret; **Bridewell Street**, after the prison (or bridewell) built in 1787; **George Lane** recalls a coaching inn; **Hyde Lane** from Sir Nicholas Hyde who was Lord Chief Justice and died in 1631; **Silverless Street** was Sylver strete in 1540 and probably takes its name from silversmithing.

The church of St Mary shows Puritan church design, being largely undecorated and open. A national subscription paid for its rebuilding after a fire in 1653.

Barton Farm was Barton in 1198 and is derived from beretun, which is Saxon for the barley settlement. Farms named Barton were frequently found close to the centres of estates. **Broadleaze** is the large pasture, from the two Saxon words brad and laes.

Isbury, on the edge of the Savernake Forest, probably means the burg (fort) on the efes (edge, border). There was a Roman settlement there and the name could refer to this.

❋ MARSTON, MARSTON MAISEY and SOUTH MARSTON

Called Merstone in 1309, it is derived from a Saxon name mersctun (marsh settlement). In 1306 it was Merston juxta Poterne, to give a clearer idea of its location. By 1559 it had become Marston. **Long Street** means as its name suggests the long road, while **Norney** means north of the boggy land. In this case the word ieg (island) has its other meaning of 'land bounded by water, or wetland'.

Marston Maisey. An identical meaning lies behind this place-name, recorded as Merston in 1199. Maisey is from Roger de Meysi, who owned the manor in 1212. The name Marshtone Meysi first appeared in 1302.

South Marston. Once again the Saxon name mersctun lies beneath this name first mentioned in 1242 as Merston. It was first recorded as Suthmershton in 1330.

❋ MELKSHAM

The Saxon name meolchamm described both the economy and location of this town. The meaning is land in the bend of a river where milk is produced. It was Melchesham in the Domesday Book though the 1229 spelling – Milkesham – gives a better indication of the name's actual meaning. The town later provided the name of the extensive medieval Melksham Forest.

The 15th century parish church is famous for the carving by the doorway of St Michael killing the dragon and a memorial inside commemorating a father, mother and six children lost on the Titanic. Within the town **Church Street** was so called – in the form Cherchestret – as early as 1370. **Praters Lane** takes its name from William Prater who lived in the area in 1642.

Beanacre means, as the name suggests, field where beans grow. In this name the Saxon word aecre has its orginal meaning of field, rather than the later meaning of a specific area measurement.

Berryfield looks to have an obvious meaning but the form recorded in 1286 – Bereghfeld – reveals that instead of 'berries' the feld (open country) was notable for its beorg (burial mound).

Blackmore Forest, called simply Blakemor in 1230, is so named because it was within the medieval Melksham Forest. The first part means black marshy land.

Rhotteridge Farm is the red ridge and was Raderygge in 1331. Why this colour was chosen for the place-name is something of a mystery.

Shaw is derived from the Saxon word sceage, which was used of a copse and also of underwood used as a field border. It was first recorded in 1256 as Schawe. A more familiar spelling – Shawe juxta Melksham – had emerged by 1379. **Soho Farm** is a joking reference to its distance from the heart of the parish. This is one of a number of Wiltshire uses of London as a measurement of distance.

Whitley means the white leah (either clearing, or its earlier meaning of wood). **Woolmore Farm** has nothing to do with sheep but rather refers to wolves. The 1249 spelling – Wolvemere – shows that it derives from the Saxon for pool of the wolves.

✽ MERE

The modern name is identical in spelling to that recorded in the Domesday Book, though later medieval spellings in 1316 (Mayre) and 1337 (Miere) reveal how changeable place-name forms can be. The name is probably from the Saxon word gemaere (boundary) as it is near the Wiltshire, Somerset, Dorset borders; though it may derive from the Saxon word mere (lake).

In the town **Boar Street** was originally Bore Streat in 1574 and the names of **Castle Street**, **Church Street**, **Salisbury Street**, **Water Street** and **Wet Lane** have all remained virtually unchanged since at least the 16th century. The inn the **Old Ship**, once called Sign of the Ship, takes its name from the badge of John Mere who founded a chantry in the church in the 14th century. The present house – dating from the 17th century – was once the home of Sir John Coventry. The unfortunate Sir John, who had antagonised Charles II by attacking his immorality, was in 1670 victim of a brutal attack in a London street which left his nostrils slit open. The crime prompted Parliament to pass the so-called Coventry Act which imposed the death penalty for such mutilations.

The church of St Michael is dominated by a huge 15th century tower and within by a fine 15th century rood screen.

Barrow Street means the roadway by the beorg (burial mound) and was referred to in 1285 as la Baruwe. The version Barowstreate appeared in 1566. **Burton** is from the Saxon name burgtun (settlement by the fort, or in this case town). It was Burinton in 1204.

Chaddenwick means the wic (dairy farm) belonging to Ceadela and is a Saxon name. **Horsington Lane** either takes its name from Henry de Horsington who lived here in 1305, or from Horsington in south Somerset. It is possible that the Somerset place-name gave rise to the personal-name, which in turn led to this minor name being coined.

Knowl was cnol in 956 and means the small hill. The name is Saxon.

❧ MILDENHALL

The meaning of this place-name is Milda's hollow, from the name of an otherwise unknown Saxon landowner and halh (hollow). The spelling of this name in 803 – Mildanhald – is not greatly different from the modern name, though spellings in 1539 (Midnall) and 1760 (Minal) reflect local pronunciation.

The curious name **Cock-a-troop Cottages** dates from at least 1257, when the spelling Crokerestrope reveals the meaning as the thorp (hamlet) of the crocker (potter). This last word is also found in the name Crockerton. The pottery in question is probably Roman pottery excavated locally, as the large Roman settlement of Cunetio occupied the site. Near the cottages is **Black Field** probably named from the ancient debris turned up by the plough. In 1578 it was Blacke fyeld, showing how long its distinctive character has been known.

Elcot was spelled in exactly this way in 1237, though later in 1257 it was Ellecote and in 1331 Elescote extra Marlebergh. It means the cot (cottage) by the elder tree and is a Saxon name.

Folly Copse probably refers to unproductive land, while **Oxleaze Copse** means the wood next to the laes (pasture) where oxen graze. **Poulton** is the tun (settlement) by the pol (pool, pond). The name was first

recorded in the Domesday Book as Poltone. By 1625 it had become Poul-
ten.

Sound Copse takes its name from a Saxon word for 'safety' and may have
been chosen because the valley was particularly sheltered. **Stitchcombe**
was Stotecome in the Domesday Book and is Stut's cumb (short, broad
valley). In 1574 it was a recognisable Stichcombe.

❋ MILSTON

Called Mildestone in the Domesday Book, the name means the middle-
most settlement, from the common Saxon word tun (settlement) and
midlesta. By 1309 it had become Milleston and the modern spelling con-
tinues this development, making it look as if the name should refer to a
mill, which it does not.

Brigmerston was Brismartone in the Domesday Book and means the
tun (settlement) of someone with a name like Brismar.

❋ MILTON LILBOURNE

Although it looks as if it should have a meaning related to mills the 1198
spelling – Middelton – reveals that this is not the case. In fact the name
means middle settlement, derived from the Saxon middeltun. As late as
1271 it was called Mydilton but by 1412 the spelling Milton had predominated. Lilbourne is from Walter de Lillebon who owned the manor in
1242. This place, near Pewsey, is sometimes confused with Middleton in
Warminster Hundred. **Clay Lane** in the village has carried this name since
at least 1628, when it was called East and West Cley.

Fyfield, called fifide in 1230, means the five hides. A hide was a Saxon
measurement of land. Five hides were thought sufficient to provide for
the needs of the lowest class of thegn, a Saxon aristocrat. Richer thegns
owned significantly more land than this.

Giant's Grave is one of a number of Wiltshire burial mounds where there
is a local legend that the mound is inhabited by a giant. In this case the
site is a long barrow, dating from the New Stone Age. A local legend claims
that if the mound is run round seven times then the giant will appear.

The long barrow is built of chalk and 90m long. When it was excavated in the 19th century it was found to contain the remains of three or four people at its eastern end. One of these had died from a blow to the head. A leaf-shaped arrowhead was also found.

Little Salisbury is a nickname for a small settlement. An interesting attempt to make sense of an ancient name lies behind **Milkhouse Water**. The name actually means cottages by the mill. This is obvious from 1257 when it was named Milecote. What lies behind it is a Saxon name mylncot. The modern form is an attempt to interpret a name coined in a language no longer used.

Totteridge Farm was Tetherigg in 1199 and means the tote (lookout) hrycg (ridge); both words are Saxon.

❉ MINETY

This means the mint island and was spelled Mintig in 844. It comes from two Saxon words minte (mint) and eg (island). Wiltshire Wildlife Trust own two reserves in the vicinity of Minety. **Distillery Farm Meadows** has rich meadowland and is famous for its colourful meadow flowers which are at their best in May, June and July. It is typical of what the 19th century writer, William Cobbett, described as the 'cheese' country of Wiltshire. This was the dairying clay lowlands in contrast to the 'chalk', the downland grazed by sheep. At nearby **Emmett Hill Meadows** another traditional hay meadow is preserved. The name Emmett is from a dialect word for ants, yet there are now very few anthills there. Perhaps in the past they were more plentiful here. **Long Meadow** has heath spotted orchid and meadow thistle growing there, while the field called **Pignut** is not surprisingly white with pignut flowers in May and June. These support chimney sweeper moths, whose caterpillars feed on the leaves.

Brandier is a dialect word more usual in the north and meaning a gridiron. It probably was applied here to a pattern of ridge and furrow in the ploughed open fields.

Brownockhill means brown oak hill. This sense is conveyed by the 1591 spelling, Browning Oke.

·· N ··

❧ NETHERAVON

The Domesday Book spelling – Nigravre – gives few clues that this name derives from a Saxon name, neotheravon, which means the lower place on the river Avon. The river-name is Welsh and means river. By 1212 the place-name had developed into the more recognisable spelling, Netheraven. The church here is mostly 13th century but the tower survives from Saxon times.

The Folly is another example of the name for disappointing land. **Great Lynch** contains the Saxon word hlinc. This had a range of meanings including bank, terraced hill and hill slope.

Newfoundland Farm is so named in 1820 and – being in a distant corner of the parish – probably takes its name from a joking reference to a remote place, in this case Newfoundland, Canada.

A very interesting name is that of **Robin Hood Ball**. The reference is probably to a mound, or burial mound. The reference to Robin Hood arises from the popularity of the medieval story of the outlaw.

Wexland refers to land where bees' wax was collected.

❧ NETHERHAMPTON

The Saxon word neothera (lower) also lies behind the first half of this name. The second element is also Saxon and is either the word haematun (settlement of the people), or perhaps hamtun, used in the sense home-farm/main farm of an estate. Together they have a meaning like people of the lower village, or the lower home farm. The name was Notherhampton in 1242 and Netherhampton in 1249.

Upper Folly may refer to land with a disappointing yield and is a fairly common minor name in Wiltshire.

❧ NETTLETON

First recorded as Netelintone, in 944, this means nettle settlement, from Saxon netele and tun. Clearly the plant grew in some numbers here. In the Domesday Book it was Niteletone, Nettelinctone in 1235 and Netelton in 1242. **Marsh Lane** was first mentioned in 1562 as le Mershe, when **Wood Lane** was Wodestrete (Woodstreet). The church of St Mary is famous for its tower adorned with elegant windows and pinnacles. The upper stages are entirely covered with tracery and one of the bells is about 500 years old. Georgian box pews fill the nave and the church is also notable for the stairway built into the thickness of the wall, which gives the preacher access to the pulpit.

The areas of this straggling village are differentiated by the names **Nettleton Green** and **Nettleton Shrub**. The latter may be as old as the Saxon word scrybb (shrub), or more modern as the word, with changed spelling, has continued in use to the present day.

Burton is derived from a Saxon original burgtun (the fortified settlement). **Fosse Farm** takes its name from the nearby Roman road, called the Fosse Way.

Hatch was Hache in 1289 and comes from the Saxon word haecc. This can be translated as a gate, floodgate, sluice. The name can be used of situations as different as a gate into a forest and a fish weir. The former may be more likely here.

Long Dean is from the Saxon langdenu (long and large valley). **Lugbury** contains the Saxon word burg (fort) but actually refers to a long barrow burial mound of the New Stone Age. This barrow is 58m long, 27m wide and 2m high. When excavated it was found to contain four sealed burial chambers on the south side. In these were 26 skeletons, of which ten were bodies of children. Another skeleton – in a crouched position – was discovered near the eastern end of the mound.

Priory Farm refers to land which once belonged to Malmesbury Abbey. **Woodford Brake** is an ancient name and was Wodeford in a charter of 944. The modern spelling exactly represents its meaning and shows how some words have continued in use with little change for over a millennium.

❊ NEWNTON, LONG

In a charter of 681 this was plain Niuentun, meaning the new settlement, from the Saxon words neowa and tun. It was Newenton in the Domesday Book. 'Long' is a later addition, not recorded until 1331, when it was called Long Newenton. As late as 1571 it was sometimes referred to as Newnton alias Longe Newnton.

The second element in **Boldridge** is derived from the Saxon word hrycg, though the word has continued into modern usage. The first element may be a number of Saxon words: bold (house/palace), bothl (homestead), boulder (bullrush). It is hard to be certain, though the last possibility is least likely.

The Folly is a fairly common name and often must have referred to disappointing land.

❊ NEWNTON, NORTH

This is the north new settlement, from a Saxon name northneowatun. It is north of Upavon. It was Northniwetune in 892, Newetone in the Domesday Book and Northneuton in 1242.

Butts Farm probably refers to medieval archery. **Cuttenham Farm** probably takes its name from the Saxon personal name Cotta and hamm (land in the bend of a river). It was first mentioned in 1315.

The strangely named **Cats Brain** has no reference to cats. Instead it is a dialect word which was used to describe coarse soil made up of clay and stones.

A series of right-angled bends in the parish boundary inspired the name of **Gores**. It is derived from the Saxon word gara (angle). It was lez Goores in 1570.

Hilcott was called Hulcot in 1196 and comes from a Saxon word hulucot (a shed). This may have referred to a poor, or very basic, human dwelling or a shelter for animals.

❧ NEWTON, SOUTH

The original meaning of this name was simply the new settlement. This is apparent in a reference to it in a charter of 943 as Niwantune. By 1242 it had become Sutneuton and this stuck; though in 1312 it was briefly called Niweton juxta Wilton (Newton near Wilton).

Chilhampton contains the Saxon word cilda (children) but in this case it probably refers to young servants responsible for running the farmstead here, or possibly young noblemen.

Folly Farm is a common minor name for disappointing land.

Little Wishford was plain Wicheford in the Domesday Book and comes from two Saxon words which combined mean the ford where wych-elm grows. It was Parva Whicheford, in 1316 and Litel Wycford – with the same meaning – in 1324.

Stoford means the stony ford and is first recorded in 943 as Stanford.

❧ NEWTON TONY

This is yet another new settlement and called Newentone in the Domesday Book. Tony is from the family name Toeni. This family came originally from Tosny in France. Later landowners – the Malets – are commemorated in the 19th century church. Above one tablet hangs the sword of George Malet. He died in 1856 fighting in Persia.

Cleve Hill contains the Saxon word clif (steep slope, cliff). **Wilbury House** takes its name from Wilbury Hill and contains the Saxon word burg (camp) referring to a probable prehistoric fort west of the house.

❧ NO MAN'S LAND

This very unusually named place is close to the border with Hampshire. It is first recorded in 1817 and may take its name from the fact that it appeared to lie between the two counties.

❈ NORTON

Sited north of Hullavington the name means north settlement and is Saxon. It was first mentioned in 937 as Nortun.

Bucklands Farm may take its name from an 18th century local family, or the family may have taken the place's name. In this case the name may represent a Saxon bocland (estate given by a charter).

The unusual field-name **Ellstub** is first mentioned in 931 and comes from a Saxon original ellernstubb, meaning the stump of the elder-tree.

Gorsey Leaze is probably the pasture where gorse grows. The word Leaze ultimately derives from the Saxon word laes. However, the name may not necessarily be ancient as the use of the term leaze for pasture continued well after the Anglo-Saxon period.

Maidford takes its name not from a young woman but instead from the Saxon word magthe (mayweed).

❈ NORTON BAVANT

Yet another north settlement and called Nortone in the Domesday Book. Bavant is from Roger Bavent, who owned the manor in 1344. The hamlet is north-east of Sutton Veny.

Cotley Hill may be the leah (clearing) where a cot (cottage) was built. However, without an early spelling it is difficult to be absolutely sure that it is derived from these two Saxon words.

Middleton was Mideltone in the Domesday Book and comes from the Saxon words for the middle tun (settlement).

Above the settlement, which is located in the Wylye valley, is **Scratchbury Camp**, a prehistoric hillfort. Scratch is a West Country name for the Devil and the name may have arisen because the old hillfort dated from pagan times. The earth banks are over a mile round and enclose an area of 15ha. Inside the ramparts are Bronze Age burial mounds. Two lie inside the fort, by the north-east entrance. A cremated body was discovered in one of these. Another burial mound lies in the south-west corner.

This is of the type known from its shape as a bowl barrow, and is 30m in diameter and 3m high. When excavated in 1802 it was found to contain animal bones and burnt stones but no discernible body. Another barrow was also excavated on the same day and this lay in the centre of the fort. Inside it were buried a bronze dagger, a bronze pin, amber beads and an amber ring.

❀ OAKSEY

This place-name, contrary to its appearance, has nothing to do with oak trees. It actually means Wocc's island, from the name of an otherwise unrecorded landowner and the Saxon word ieg (a West Saxon form of eg, meaning island). The meaning is clearer in the Domesday Book spelling, Wochesie. This survived into the 16th century, after which spellings such as Okyssey (1535) and Oxey (1585) appear. A throwback to the original pronunciation can be found in the 1620 version – Okesey alias Woxy.

Clattingar was Clothangare in 1332 and Cladhangre in 1337. It derives from two Saxon words clate (burdock) and hangra (slope). The meaning is the slope where burdock grows.

Church Farm may either come from the name of the 'atte Church' family which lived here in the 14th century, or more likely was church property which gave rise to the local surname.

Dean Farm was Netherdene in 1347 and Overdene in 1568. The name comes from the Saxon word denu (large valley). The version containing 'nether' means lower. The fact that there is also a settlement named 'over' may suggest that originally there were two farms in the area now represented by one, Dean Farm. However the Saxon word 'neothera' (lower) can sometimes be corrupted to 'eothera' and then 'othera' in place-names. This is seen in another Wiltshire place-name, Netherhampton which was written Otherhampton in 1208. If this happened with Netherdene it is possible that the 1568 spelling does not in fact represent another settlement, but simply a version of the name Netherdene which, because it had become Otherdene, was corrupted to Overdene and thus gained an entirely new (and incorrect) meaning.

Moor Farm originally had the much longer name of Wokhamesmore in 1568 and also shows the real meaning of Oaksey, discussed above. This means the wild land belonging to Oaksey.

Norwood is actually the north wood and a 14th century spelling, Northwode, makes this very clear.

Strikingly named **Sodom Farm** was actually Sarhams in 1816 and probably means the sear (withered) hamm (land in the bend of a river, meadow).

Woodfolds Farm was Woodfeldes in 1568 and means the open land by the wood. Alternatively, it may mean arable land by the wood as, from the 10th century, the Saxon word feld (open country) also came to be used of once open country broken in for crops, hence our modern word 'field'.

❧ ODSTOCK

This is Oda's outlying farm, from a Saxon original Odastoc. Its pronunciation has not changed much in a millennium. It was Odestoche in the Domesday Book, Odestoke in 1372 and Oddestock in 1281. Interestingly, in the Domesday Book it was originally written as Odestote but then corrected. A record, dating from 1732, reveals that it was occasionally called Adstocke. It is now famous for its large hospital.

The **Yew Tree Inn** has traditionally been the meeting point of gipsies commemorating the anniversary of the hanging of the gipsy Joshua Scamp, in 1801, who was wrongfully accused of horse stealing.

Great Yews Wood was called The Yew Trees in 1693 and Yew Bushes in 1720. **Snakesfield Plantation** clearly refers to land infested by snakes and has had this reputation since at least 1674.

❋ OGBOURNE (ST ANDREW and ST GEORGE)

Ocheburne in Domesday Book, the name means Occa's stream, from the Saxon name Occa and the word burna. The second part of each name is from the local church dedication, first recorded in both cases in 1332. Earlier, Ogbourne St George was called Ocheburna magna (Great Ogbourne) and Ogbourne St Andrew was Ocheburna parva (Little Ogbourne) in 1143 and on other occasions but the church dedications replaced these alternative names.

At **Ogbourne St Andrew** there are a number of other interesting names. **Bay Bridge** takes its name from an artificial lake called Baylake, first mentioned in 1547. Bay means dam and the lake formed behind it was also called the King's Great Stew.

Castle Farm refers to nearby Barbury Castle, an Iron Age hillfort (see Wroughton). **Poughcombe** was Pokcombe and means goblin valley from the Saxon word puca. **Rockley** is the clearing, or wood, of the rooks. The Saxon word leah can mean both wood and clearing. In 1591 it was called Templerookley, as the land here had once been owned by the crusading order of the Knights Templar. **Smeathe's Plantation** is not a corruption of smith but represents the Saxon word smethe (smooth). **Temple Bottom** refers to land owned by the Knights Templar, already mentioned in connection with Rockley. In the churchyard at Ogbourne St Andrew stands a round barrow which was later turned into a Norman motte-and-bailey castle. A local tradition claimed that the burial mound was infested by vipers, perhaps because the mound was pagan and the snakes would be symbols of evil. The close proximity of the church may suggest it was built here to Christianise a site associated with pagan beliefs. The church itself is Norman.

Ogbourne Maizey is a hamlet in the parish of **Ogbourne St George** and takes its name from Robert de Meysey who owned land here in 1242. Other names nearby include **Bytham Farm** which contains the Saxon word bytme (bottom, a landscape feature); **Church Hill** has been called this since at least 1496 when it was Chirchehyll; **Herdswick Farm** possibly means wic (dairy farm) by the haes (a beech, or oak wood), both words are Saxon; **Woolmer Farm** is actually Saxon for the wolves' pool and appears in a record of 1339 as Wolvemere.

❧ ORCHESTON (ST GEORGE and ST MARY)

Each name means Ordric's settlement, from the Saxon name Ordric and the common word tun, to be found in many Wiltshire place-names. The second part of each name is from the local church dedication, first recorded in the case of Orcheston St George in 1279 (Orcheston Seynt Jorge) and for Orcheston St Mary in 1524 (Orston Mary). Both settlements were combined in the Domesday Book name of Orcestone and probably originally formed two parts of one estate. Orcheston St George was called Orcheston Boyvile in 1291 after Henry de Bovile who had earlier owned land there.

Thomas Goddard 1517

110

At **Orcheston St George** there are a number of other interesting place-names. **Elston** takes its name from Elias Giffard, a landowner in the 12th century and shows that the Saxon word 'tun' (settlement) was used to make place-names well after the Norman Conquest in 1066. **Cozen's Farm** recalls a 14th century landowner here. **The Cleeve** contains the Saxon word clif (cliff, steep slope). **Honeydown Ridge** probably refers to a reputation for honey being found in the area. **Silver Barrow** has been called this since at least the early 19th century and probably refers to some local legend about treasure hidden in a burial mound. Such traditions are common across the country and a number of such legends survive from different places in Wiltshire.

Near **Orcheston St Mary** the place-name **Rolleston** takes its name from an otherwise unknown 12th century landowner named Rolf. Like Elston is shows a very late use of the word tun. Before this it was called Wintreburne, as were a number of nearby manors.

❉ OVERTON, WEST

The 939 spelling, Uferantune, shows that this probably means upper settlement, from two Saxon words ufera (upper) and tun (settlement). It is possible that it means settlement near the river bank/border, from the Saxon word ofer. It is near the river Kennet and the same charter of 939 also calls it Ofertunes. In 1316 it was called Ouertun Abbatisse as it was then owned by the Abbess of Wilton. The name Westovertone first appears in 1275.

On **Overton Hill** there is a barrow cemetery consisting of about a dozen Bronze Age round barrows. The old name for the hill was Seofan Beorgas, which means seven barrows. In the 17th century the name survived as Seven Barrowes Hill. The fact that there are clearly more than seven barrows on the hill may suggest that the number seven was chosen because often this number is accorded a mystical significance and suggests something unusual, or supernatural. Excavations here revealed a burial in a tree-trunk coffin together with an axe and bronze dagger.

A prehistoric circle – now referred to as the Sanctuary – once lay on Overton Hill and from here a ceremonial avenue led down to the prehistoric site at Avebury. The circle was destroyed in the 18th century and rediscovered in the 1930s. There were two stone circles and six concentric rings of post-holes. These seem to represent a number of successive timber buildings, the last of which was surrounded by two stone circles. Now all that can be seen are concrete posts marking the positions of the stones and wooden posts.

Boreham Wood was Borham in 1249 and probably means in the Saxon language the ham (home) of the gebur (a class of peasant). The word ham is rare in Wiltshire, where the word tun is more frequently used of settlements. Ham is more common in the east of England. Both ham and tun were used of a range of settlements from farms up to villages. In the case of Boreham the word ham is used in the sense that it eventually developed of a 'home' and our modern word derives from the Saxon original. Incidentally the word tun developed into our modern word town.

East Overton is a small settlement within the parish of West Overton and in 1167 was called Ouertun Prioris because it belonged to the church of St Swithin's, Winchester.

Fosbury is first recorded in 1270 as Fortesbyria and means either the forst (roof) burg (fort) in the sense of elevated fort, or it may mean the forworst (chieftain) burg (fort). All the possible words are Saxon.

Grey Wethers is first mentioned in 1721 and refers to sarsen stones found here which look like sheep (wethers).

Henley Wood derives from a Saxon original heahleah (high wood) in which leah is used in its older sense of 'wood' rather than the sense that it developed during the Saxon period, 'clearing'.

Hursley Bottom is in Saxon the hyrs (mare) leah (clearing). This is clear in the spelling recorded in 939 of Hyrsleage. **Lockeridge** comes from the Saxon name locahrycg (enclosures on the ridge).

Pickledean is first mentioned in 939 as Pytteldene and derives from two Saxon words meaning the denu (valley) of the pyttel (mouse-hawk). **Pumphrey Wood** takes its name from an 18th century tenant.

Shaw Farm contains the Saxon word sceaga, which means a copse. **West Overton Down** first appears in a Latin form in 1348, super montem de Overton, which gives it a very grand sound. **Wools Grove** has nothing to do with sheep but means Wulfsige's grove.

·· P ··

❀ PATNEY

Mentioned in 963 as Peatanige, the name means literally Peatta's ieg (island). However as well as 'island', this Saxon word can mean dry land bounded by marsh and well watered land. Either of these options is most likely to be the meaning here.

❀ PEWSEY

This name means Pefe's island. It is derived from a Saxon name, Pefe and the word eg (island). This word can mean dry ground rather than land in the middle of water. The place was called Pefesigge in 880, Pevesie in the Domesday Book and Pewse in 1524. A statue of King Alfred stands at the centre of the town and is a reminder that he owned land here. The 700 year old church is noteworthy for the additions made to it by Canon Bouverie, rector here c1900. These include the altar and altar rail, wall paintings, the wooden cover of the font and figures in the church. **Bouverie Hall** takes its name from Canon Bouverie.

Martinsell Hill, known locally as Martinsell, was Mattelesore in 1257 and the second part of the name comes from the Saxon word ora (bank). The first part is probably a Saxon personal name. This place was once the site of a Palm Sunday Fair, famous for its sports and games. Oranges were chased down the slope but the most unusual entertainment consisted of sliding down the slope seated on the skulls or jawbones of horses. The fair gained a reputation for rowdiness and it ended around 1860. For some time after this a church service accompanied by a brass band took place here.

❀ PEWSHAM

Called Peuisham in 1448 the name probably means the hamm (land in the bend of a river) by a river called the Pew. This river-name is no longer in use.

Loxwell was Lokeswell in 1158, the wiell (spring) belonging to a Saxon named Locc. **Nethermore** is the lower mor (wild land, marshy land). **Nockets Hill** probably comes from a Saxon word which means the group of oak trees.

Rooks Nest Farm takes its name from what must have been a prominent rookery and has been called this since at least the middle of the 19th century.

❧ POOLE KEYNES

The spelling of the first word is reminiscent of Poole in Dorset and both derive from the Saxon word pol, meaning pool. In this case the reference was to a much smaller patch of water than Poole Harbour! Keynes is from Sir John Keynes who married the eldest daughter of the 14th century lord of the manor. The name first appeared in 931 as Pole. In 1610 it was recorded as Pole Canes.

Oak Well means the oak stream, or possibly well and was first recorded in 1591.

❧ POTTERNE

The Domesday Book spelling, Poterne, reveals the meaning to be pot-ters' house, from Saxon potteraern. The spelling with double 't' (but minus the 'e') first appears in 1281. **Wallen Lane** in the village was Walelond in 1422. The name is Saxon, meaning the land of the wealas (the Welsh speakers). A field nearby was called Wallands in the 1840s.

The Butts would take its name from medieval archery practice and is a common name, found in a number of different places.

Byde Farm is an abbreviation of the 1341 version, Bidesknappe and means literally by the cnaepp (small hill). **Cadley Farm** is the leah (clearing) of Cada, an otherwise unknown Saxon landowner.

Furzehill is a hill shaped like a ridge or roof. The area was Forsthull in 1225. **Potterne Field** is the feld (open land) belonging to Potterne and probably goes back to a Saxon original. It was Poternewike in 1203. **Potterne Wick** is so called because it would have been a secondary settlement belonging to Potterne. The Saxon word wic has a number of meanings but in this case it probably meant dairy farm. It is recorded as Poternewike in 1203.

Sleight Farm derives from a Saxon word for a sheep walk, or grazing area. **Stroud Hill** contains the Saxon word strod, a word used for wet land. **Whistley Farm** is the damp meadow in the leah (clearing).

❧ POULSHOT

The name is derived from the Saxon Paul's holt. A holt was a Saxon word for wood, often used for one in which a single tree species predominated. The place was Paveshou in the Domesday Book and Paulesholt in 1187. **Leighball Lane** means the clearing by the earth landmark.

Summerham Bridge is from hamm (land in the bend of a river) used in the summer.

❧ PRESHUTE

This is a difficult name to decipher. It was Prestcheta in 1185, Preschute in 1252 and Pershute in 1321. The first part is almost certainly the Saxon word preost (priest). However, the second element could be a British word, ceto, Welsh coed (wood), or a Saxon word, ciete (cottage/cell). The chalk horse on the hill above the river was first cut in 1804 by school-boys from Marlborough College. The black marble font in the church came, according to local tradition, from Marlborough Castle. In the 16th century the antiquarian Camden noted that the local people boasted that it had seen the baptism of princes.

Nearby **Clatford** is identical with its Domesday Book spelling and means ford where the clate (water-lily) grows. The word is Saxon as is the name **Manton**. This means Manna's tun (farm), or the tun of Manna's people.

Devil's Den is a prehistoric burial chamber. It is probably called this because of its pagan origins.

Granham Farm was Grendon in the 13th century and means the green hill. It is derived from a Saxon original.

Shoulder of Mutton Plantation quite clearly takes its name not from sheep farming but from the shape of the woodland.

❧ PURTON

The name is a survival of Saxon fruit growing, as it means pear-tree orchard, from Saxon pirige (pear) and tun. In this name, tun is probably used in its earliest sense of enclosure, rather than settlement. The name is first recorded in 796 as Puritone. The shorter form of the name does not appear until 1211, in the form Pertune. However, as late as 1580 the slightly longer form was remembered and the village was called Pyrton alias Puryton.

The painting of the Last Supper in the church may be by a pupil of Rubens and the font was once used as a horse trough – after its removal in 1807 and before being restored to its place within the church.

Hog's Lane in the village has carried this name since 1257. **Smithmead Lane** means the smooth meadow, from a Saxon word smethe. The village is unusual in having no less than four war memorials; each one of which states different casualty figures. The pub **The Ghost Train** is named after a railway station, shut in the 1960s.

Abbots Bridge takes its name from the Abbot of Malmesbury who owned land here and the bridge has been so called since at least 1553 and obviously earlier than this as monastic houses had been dissolved by Henry VIII before this date.

Battle Lake is a curious name suggesting a local legend about some kind of conflict in the area. What this tradition was remains a mystery but it survives in this minor name.

Bentham derives from the Saxon words beonet (bent grass) hamm (land in the bend of a river).

Bremell Farm almost certainly takes its name from the Saxon word bremel (bramble). Clearly the area must have had them in noticeable amounts. **Brockhurst Farm** was Brokouere in 796 revealing the fact that it came from the Saxon brocyfer (brook slope). The sense is a slope near a brook.

Purton Church

Bury Hill is the burg (fort) hill, the name coming from a prehistoric fort.

Clardon House was recorded in 1400 as Claverdon and is from a Saxon name meaning clover hill.

College Farm is so called because it belonged to Worcester College. **Haxmore Farm** is the wild land where coarse grass grows and contains two Saxon words, hassuc – from which comes the modern word for a clump of grass, hassock – and mor. It first appears in the records in 796 as Hassukes mor. **Hursted Farm** was Hursteeds Close in 1630 and means in Saxon the hus (house) stede (site, place of). It must have referred to a particular dwelling place, possibly a small farm.

Paven Hill may contain a Saxon personal name but the appearance of the word has been affected by the fact that a Roman mosaic pavement was found here, which is why it now looks similar to 'pavement hill'. In the 13th century it was Pevenhull which looks somewhat different. This shows how a place-name can be adjusted in order to make it appear to make sense, even when this distorts the original form and meaning.

Purton Stoke means the stoc (secondary settlement) dependent on Purton and in the Domesday Book was plain Stoche. **Restrop** seems to contain a Saxon personal name attached to the word throp (village). **Ringsbury Camp** means the circular burg (fort).

·· R ··

❧ RAMSBURY

Ramsbury gives its name to the other bishop in Wiltshire; the senior and more famous being, of course, the Bishop of Salisbury. The place was called Rammesburi in 947, meaning the raven's fort, from a Saxon original, hraefnburg. The first element could be a personal name; however a Latin form of the place-name, recorded in 905 as Corvinensis, suggests it is the name of the bird. A bishopric was established at Ramsbury in the 10th century but was later united with Sherborne, in 1058. Later the Wiltshire bishopric became centred on Salisbury. In recent years the title has been re-established.

The Crown and Anchor in the village was the Crown in 1878 but many of the street-names are much older. **Oxford Street** was Oxenfordstrete in 1331 while **High Street** was first recorded in 1570. In the church there are two noteworthy coped tombstones which are Saxon, dating from the 9th century. The goblet-shaped font is decorated with carvings of fishes and has Biblical scenes on the stem. The latter were carved in the 18th century.

Axford was Axeford in 1184 but Assheford in 1289. It means the ford of the ash trees, as is clear from the 1289 spelling. It has nothing to do with axes.

Hilldrop was Hullethorp in 1310 and means the hill thorp (hamlet). It had developed into Hildrop by 1510. **Knighton** as it may appear was the tun (settlement) of the knights. However the Saxon word cniht meant serving man and did not have the higher class status that the word assumed in the later Middle Ages. **Littlecot** means, as it appears to, the little cottage and is from a Saxon original.

Membury was called Minbiry in 1090 and contains the Welsh word min (edge) and the Saxon word burg (fort). The meaning is fort on the edge; in this case the edge of high ground.

Thrup Farm takes its name from the Saxon word thorp (hamlet). It was Thrope in 1478. **Whittonditch** was Whitedic in 1249, which reveals its origin in the Saxon for white ditch.

Amongst the woodland names scattered across the very large parish (its bounds stretch some 26 miles!) are **Cocked Hat Coppice** and **Leg of Mutton Copse** named from the unusual shape of the woodland. Cocked Hat Coppice was also called Three Corner Clump. **Bower Wood** may contain the Saxon word gebur, referring to a class of peasant. **Paxlet Plantation** means Paecci's slaed (short valley). **Foxley Wood** means clearing, or wood, frequented by foxes. **Hens Wood** was Hensedd in 1570 and may have its origins in two Saxon words, henn (wild bird) and secg (sedge).

❋ REDLYNCH

First recorded as Radelynch in 1282, the name means the red bank, from two Saxon words read (red) and hlinc (ridge/bank). By the 16th century the name was spelled Redlynche. **Newhouse** at Redlynch is thought to have been built early in the 17th century and was enlarged later in that century and the 18th century. The house is home to a collection of artifacts connected with Admiral Nelson.

Bishop's Wood belonged to the Bishop of Winchester and was once Church land. The unusually named **Bohemia** is in a remote corner of the parish and is a humorous name. **Hamptworth** comes from the Saxon name haematunworth and means homestead belonging to the village of the people.

Pensworth also contains the Saxon word worth (homestead) but in this case linked to the personal name Pendel. Why a London suburb should be taken as the name of **Pimlico Firs** is a mystery. **Radnor Firs** takes its name from the landowning aristocrat, the Earl of Radnor.

❧ ROLLESTON

Actually called Wintreburne in the Domesday Book, this became Rolveston by 1242. It means the tun (settlement) belonging to Rolf. It is an example of how the Saxon word 'tun' continued to be used to make place-names for some time after the Norman Conquest.

❧ ROUNDWAY

Roundway Down, above the village, was the site of a bloody Civil War battle, fought in 1643. The village name first appears, in the form Rindweiam, in 1149. It comes from the Saxon rymed (cleared) weg (road). By 1493 it was appearing as Rundewey and by 1619 a more familiar spelling of Roundwaye had developed. According to local legends the burial mounds on **Roundway Down** are haunted by a black dog with a rattling chain. In some traditions such dogs were supposed to protect the dead – in this case presumably those in the barrows – from harm.

Nursteed was Nutstede in 1249 and means the stede (site, place) where nuts grow. **Wick Green** takes its name from the Saxon word wic which was generally used to denote a dairy farm.

❧ ROWDE

This compact, brick-built, village was first recorded in the Domesday Book as Rode. It is derived from the Saxon word rodu (clearing). In charters this word indicates a linear clearing, as opposed to the use of the commoner word leah. It is possible that the name may be from the Saxon word hreod (reed bed). The 'w' in the middle of the name first appeared during the reign of Elizabeth I. The **George and Dragon** pub dates from about 1600. A pub of a similar date stood on the site of the present **Cross Keys**, which was built in 1938 to replace the earlier building which had been destroyed by fire. Robert Trotman of Rowde died near Poole (Dorset) on a smuggling expedition in 1765 in a fight with Customs officers.

Caen Hill is famous for its flight of locks on the Kennet and Avon Canal and in 1612 went under the less continental sounding name, Canehill.

Durlett Farm is from two Saxon words thyrel (pierced) and geat (gate). Though it was spelled Durlete in 1255 the meaning is clearer in a slightly later spelling – Thurlegate. The meaning may be that of open or smooth ground through which there was easy movement.

Nine Hills was originally Lyme Hills and shows how a name can be corrupted over time.

Smithwick Farm is the smethe (smooth) wic (dairy farm). The first word may refer to flat ground. Both words are Saxon. **Wick Farm** derives from the Saxon word wic (dairy farm). In the 14th century it was Roudewyk, meaning the wic belonging to Rowde.

❧ RUSTHALL

Recorded in the Domesday Book as Rusteselve this place-name probably means rust coloured secluded piece of land. The two Saxon words behind the name are rust and healh. The former is a difficult word to decipher. There may have been a Saxon personal name, Rusta. In this case the meaning would be Rusta's secluded piece of land. Alternatively the first element may be hrost, which meant 'perch', or 'roost'. All in all a complex name. By 1416 the name was spelled Rosshall and in 1627 Rushall alias Rustehall.

Nearby **France Farm** is so named, according to local tradition, because one has to cross water to get to it, whichever route is chosen.

Old Cleeve contains the Saxon word clif (steep place, cliff).

Slay Barrow has nothing to do with slaughter but contains a probably Saxon word meaning grassy slope.

·· S ··

❀ SALISBURY

Called Searobyrg in 552, in the *Anglo-Saxon Chronicle*, it means the armour fort, from a Saxon original searaburg. It is derived from the Romano-British name Sorviodunum, a language which is an ancestor of modern Welsh. The first element sounded like the Saxon word searu and the second also meant fort and so became burg. The first 'r' became 'l' through Norman influence. The name was first applied to the hillfort and then to the town below it. In the Domesday Book it was written Salesberia, which by 1422 had developed into Sallesbury. The present name of **Old Sarum** is a more modern attempt to differentiate the two places. The magnificent cathedral was built in the 13th century as part of a medieval new-town. The original cathedral had been within the ramparts of Old Sarum – an Iron Age hillfort. However, the exposed nature of the site, as well as disputes with the occupants of the castle led to a change of location.

Within the present city the ancient street-names bear witness to the past. Amongst many fascinating examples, **Blue Boar Row**, first recorded in 1751, takes its name from an even older inn. **Chipper Lane** is derived from the medieval word chiperie (place of the market-men). **Endless Street** dates from at least 1339 and was the road leading out of the city.

Barnard Street originally led to Barnard's Cross and in 1428 was called Bernewellcros, suggesting that the original cross was sited by a spring by a barn. **Butcher Row** has carried this name since at least 1339, when it was called le Bocherewe. In 1362 it was called le Potrew, which shows that at some time pots were made here as well as butchery carried out. An example of how names can change over time is provided by **Catherine Street**. This was originally Carterestrete in 1339 and meant the street of the cart makers. However by 1623 it had changed to Katherine Street and the modern name is a development of this. Another medieval trade is recorded in **Fish Row**, which was Fissherowe in 1554. The same is true of **Gigant Street** where the spelling of 1451 – Gygornestrete – shows that it derives from the Middle English word gigour meaning fiddler.

Trinity Street takes its name from the medieval Trinity Hospital which was first recorded in 1397. Later this hospital developed into alms houses.

Intriguingly **New Street** was so named in 1265 and is actually one of the oldest streets in the city! Similarly **New Canal** has been called this since at least 1751 and records a cut of the river which ran along here, prior to being covered over in the 19th century.

Not all names in the city are so ancient, **The Moon** pub was originally **The Conquered Moon** when it was opened in 1969, taking its name from the first manned moon landing.

Salisbury is sited in an area where a number of rivers meet. The **Avon** is a Welsh river-name meaning river. The **Bourne** is a Saxon river-name burna, meaning stream, usually reserved for clear streams in the chalk country. The **Nadder** is another Welsh name, meaning flowing. The original name would probably have been a British name Notr, related to Welsh nawf. The **Wylye** is also a Welsh name and means the tricky river, probably a reference to flooding. The original name was Gwili.

❧ SEAGRY

The Saxon name was secgrith and it means sedge brook. The Saxon word rith, or rithig, was used to describe a small stream. The name was Segrie in the Domesday Book. A reference to Over Seagry and Nether Seagry in 1773 suggests different focuses within the settlement area.

Nearby **Hungerdown** refers to a hill that was badly regarded because of its poor soil. Early medieval farmers had a blunter way of showing their disapproval. In 1350 it was called Shitarshull, which as it sounds, had a lavatorial meaning. However, by 1658, the later name had replaced the cruder original.

New Leaze Farm shows use of the Saxon word laes, (pasture).

❧ SEEND

Called Sinda in 1190 it means sandy place, from the Saxon word sende. Alternatively, it may be from a lost river name – Semnet. The name of the **Barge** pub reminds one of the importance of the nearby Kennet and Avon Canal.

Egypt Farm is probably a joking reference to distance from the heart of the parish. **Inmarsh** was Hennemershe in 1225 and means the marsh frequented by wild fowl. **Seend Head** contains the Saxon word heafod (meaning head) and refers to a landscape feature. **Seend Row** refers to a nearby linear hamlet.

❧ SEMINGTON

Spelled Semelton in 1249, this Saxon name progressed through Sembleton (1257), Semleton (1306) to Semington in 1470. The name means the tun (settlement) on the Semnet, a river-name.

Littleton was Lytelton in 1268 and means – as the name suggests – little tun (settlement). **Whaddon** is Saxon for woad hill and first appears in the Domesday Book as Wadone. In 1363 it was Whadone.

❧ SEMLEY

This is the leah (clearing) on the river Sem. A Saxon name, it first appears in a record of 955 as Semeleage. By 1329 it had become Semlegh.

Chaldicott's Farm was Chaldecotis in 1448 and means the cold cottage. **St Bartholomew's Hill** takes its name from a nearby Catholic church.

❧ SHALBOURNE

In the Domesday Book this was Scealdeburnan and means the shallow burna (stream).

Bagshot was Bechesgete in the Domesday Book and in Saxon means the gate belonging to Beocc.

Rivar contains the Saxon word yfer (slope) and was yfre in 931. **Starveall Farm** is a name that communicates disappointment with the productivity of the land here.

❊ SHERSTON

This was Scorranstan in 896. The meaning is stone near a steep slope, from two Saxon words scorra (steep slope) and stan (stone). The **Rattlebone Inn** takes its name from a local legend in which a Saxon warrior with the unSaxon name of John Rattlebone fought the Danes in a battle on the nearby Fosseway. He suffered a ferocious stomach wound but fought on – pressing a slab of stone against his side to prevent his bowels from gushing out!

Forlorn is an area name which suggests unproductive land.

Pinkney was Sherston Pinkeneye in 1351. It takes its name from the landowning de Pinkenny family who held land here in the 13th century.

Silk Wood is an example of an attempt to make sense of a name after linguistic changes rendered it incomprehensible to later inhabitants. The 1292 spelling was Selkwode and it probably means Seolca's wood, the name being Saxon.

Widley's Farm was Wydeleye in 1322 and means the leah (clearing) where withig (withies) are found. **Willesley** means Wifel's leah (clearing) and it was spelled Wyvelesleye in 1207. By the late 16th century it had shortened to Willesley.

❊ SHREWTON

This was originally Wintreburne in the Domesday Book but by 1232 had become Winterbourne Syreveton. In 1310 it was Sherritone. The name means the sheriff's tun (settlement). The Sheriff of Wiltshire held the manor in the Domesday Book and the later name developed from this.

Nearby **Net Down** contains the Saxon name neatun (cattle settlement) and first appeared in a record dating from 1323 as Netteton. It was Nettefeld in 1536 and downes of Net in 1599.

❊ SLAUGHTERFORD

This name has nothing to do with battles. The first recording of the name was Slachtoneford, in 1176, but a later spelling – Slaughtreford in 1343 – reveals it to mean sloe-tree ford. The original would have been a Saxon name slahthornford. By 1699 it had become Slaughterford and this spelling has stuck.

Nearby **Mercombe Wood** takes its name from the Saxon word gemaere (boundary) and is on the parish boundary. This is evidence of how old such boundaries can be.

❧ SOMERFORD, GREAT and LITTLE

Both were summed up as plain Sumerford in 939 and as this suggests the name means summer ford, probably a ford only used when summer drought lowered the level of the river Avon here. In 1268 Great Somerford was called Sumerford Mautravers after a medieval landowner but the name did not catch on. By 1409 the form Brode (large) Somerford appeared, to give way to Somerford Magna in 1588. Little Somerford was Sumerford Mauduyt in 1268 (after a landowner) but by 1681 this had become Little Somerford alias Somerford Mauditt. At **Little Somerford** is **Maunditts Park Farm**, which preserves the name of the same 13th century landowner mentioned earlier.

In the vicinity of **Great Somerford** is **Startley Farm** which was first mentioned in a charter of 688 and means the stiff clearing. The reference is probably to the quality of the wood or vegetation in the area. Nearby is **New Leaze Farm** which demonstrates the continued use of the Saxon word laes (pasture). It was first recorded in the early 17th century.

❧ SOMERFORD KEYNES

This name has an identical meaning to the above. It was Sumerford in an early reference from 683. Keynes is from William de Kahaines, who owned land here in 1211.

Shorncote was recorded in the Domesday Book as Schernecote and in 1242 as Scerncote. The name is Saxon and comes from scearncot (dung cottage). In 1198 the name was spelled Cernecot and this spelling appears occasionally until the 17th century. It probably arose out of a confusion with the name of the river Cerne.

Neigh Bridge may appear to involve horses but in fact in 1327 it was spelled le Ebrigge, though this had changed to Ney Bridge by the 16th century. The name means water bridge from the Saxon word ea (water).

✸ SOUTHWICK

The name Sudwich, recorded in 1196, and Suthwik (1249) show this to be the south dairy farm. The second element is the Saxon word wic, which has a number of meanings including subsidiary farm/dairy farm. It is south of Trowbridge.

Langham is the long hamm (land in the bend of a river) and is a Saxon name. **Pole's Hole** is a corruption of Paul's Hall, mentioned in 1773.

The curiously named **Romsey Oak Farm** on the Wingfield to Rode road takes its name from an oak which marked the parish boundary and the fact that the Abbess of Romsey owned land in the vicinity.

Scotland is probably so called because it is on the edge of the parish, the name being coined to express a sense of distance.

✸ STANDLYNCH

The meaning is stony hill and in the Domesday Book it was Staninges. The second element is the Saxon word hlinc, used here in the sense hill-slope.

Charlton is from the Saxon tun (settlement) of the ceorls (peasant freemen).

Trafalgar House is so named because the estate here was given by the government to the brother of Lord Nelson.

Witherington was Widetone in the Domesday Book and means in Saxon farm by the withies.

✸ STANTON FITZWARREN

The Domesday Book form Stantone reveals the meaning to be stone settlement, from the Saxon words stan and tun. Fitzwarren is from Fulco son of Warini, who owned the manor in 1196. It is one of three such names in Wiltshire. In this case the name refers to a large prehistoric standing stone.

Starveall Barn is a fairly common minor place-name, commenting on poor land which gave a low return for effort put in.

STANTON ST BERNARD

St Bernard is probably from a local family but remains something of a mystery.

Hareston Down derives from harstan (ancient stone). This expression described a boundary stone and such a gemerstan (boundary stone) was mentioned in an Anglo-Saxon charter here. Good pasture land inspired the name of **Milk Hill**, first recorded in 1425 as Melkhulle.

STANTON ST QUINTIN

St Quintin is from Herbert de Sancto Quintino who owned the manor in 1212. The name was plain Stantone in the Domesday Book and first appears as Staunton Quyntyn in 1317.

STAVERTON

Domesday Book records the name as Stavretone. It probably means enclosure made from stakes, from OE staefer and tun (in its earlier sense of enclosure, rather than settlement). Alternatively, it may mean stony ford settlement, from a Saxon original, stanfordtun. It is on the River Avon and is now the site of a large Nestlé factory.

Smallbrook has carried this name since at least the mid 11th century and in the Domesday Book was called Smalebroc. The reference is to a small stream. The Saxon word broc is used of the darker streams of the clay country, as opposed to the clear streams of the chalk country which are described by the word burna.

STOCKTON

In the Domesday Book the name appears in the form Stottune, which by 1166 had developed into Stoctun. The Saxon meaning is stocc (tree trunk) tun (settlement). It would appear to refer to the construction of the farm, or farms, though why this was different to other settlements is not clear.

STOURTON

The meaning of this name is the settlement on the river Stour, from the river-name and the common Saxon word tun. It was Stortone in the Domesday Book and Stourton by 1332. It is now famous for the nearby **Stourhead House**, a magnificent mansion built in 1720 and set above a lake adorned with grottoes and classical buildings. In the grounds of the house is located the old High Cross of Bristol which was brought here from Bristol in 1768. The source of the river Stour is celebrated in the name **Six Wells Bottom**.

Gasper first appears in 1280 as Gayespore and derives from the Saxon word spora (spur of land). The first element may be the Saxon word gata (goat).

Penridge Farm, **Pen Pits** both contain the Welsh word pen (head), meaning a hill. **Shave** takes its curious name from the Saxon woodland term sceaga (copse, underwood at the edge of a field). **Tucking Mill** refers to a fulling mill here.

STRATFORD-SUB-CASTLE

This was plain Stratford in 1091 though by 1397 the name had developed into subtus castrum. The original name was from the Saxon straetford and refers to where a Roman road crosses the river here. Nearby is **Old Sarum** (see **Salisbury**) hence the reference to 'castle'.

SUTTON BENGER

This is the southern settlement, from two Saxon words suth and tun. It is south of Seagry. Benger is from Berenger who was an undertenant here before 1066. The name appears as Suttune in 854. It is one of a number of such place-names in Wiltshire.

Nabal's Farm is a Saxon name and means Cnabba's spring. The spelling of the name in 1196 was Knabbewell which clearly suggests the use of the Saxon word wiell (spring). By the 18th century the name had shortened to a very recognisable Nabbols.

Oak Hill appears to be actually a corruption of Oat Hill and it is this latter spelling which first appears just before the middle of the 19th century. **Scotland Hill** may take its name from the Saxon word sceat (a strip of land, possibly land on the edge of an estate) but it is much more likely that the name indicates distance from the heart of the parish. If so, it is one of a number of such names in Wiltshire which refer to Scotland, Ireland, London etc.

✳ SUTTON MANDEVILLE

Plain Sudtone in the Domesday Book, this southern settlement is south of Teffont. Mandeville is from Robert de Mandevill who owned the manor in 1236.

Daslett means deor (animal, usually deer) slaed (short valley). **Row Ditch** combines the Saxon words ruh (rough) and dic (ditch). It was first recorded in 901 as rugan dic.

✳ SUTTON VENY

Also Sudtone in the Domesday Book, this is south of Bishopstrow. Veny is from Saxon faen, first recorded in the form Fenni Sutton in 1291, and meaning marshy. The dialect use of 'v' for 'f' is noteworthy.

Botany Farm is probably an abbreviation for Botany Bay and is used to describe a site that is distant from the heart of the parish. It is of a type with those places named Scotland, Ireland, London etc.

Iley Oak is a fascinating reminder of a key point in the history of England. This is almost certainly the place referred to in the *Anglo-Saxon Chronicle* in the year 878 as Iglea, the place where Alfred the Great camped the day before his defeat of the Viking army camped at Eddington. The camp was probably at what is now called **Eastleigh Wood**. In this place-name the Saxon word ieg (island) is probably used in the sense 'patch of high ground'.

Southleigh Wood was bosc de Suthle in 1257 and means the south wood. In this instance the Saxon word leah is used in its older sense, wood, rather than 'clearing', a meaning it developed during the Anglo-Saxon period.

❧ SWALLOWCLIFFE

This was Swealewanclif in a charter of 940 and means the clif (steep slope, cliff) where swallows are found. The Saxon word may refer to swallows or to burrowing sand martins. A high status Anglo-Saxon inhumation burial was excavated from under a burial mound here. The burial which was that of a woman probably dated from the 7th century.

Choulden Lane is also a very old name and was mentioned in 940 as chealfa dune. It comes from two Saxon words meaning calves' hill.

❧ SWINDON

This now major settlement has a name meaning pig hill, from Saxon swin (swine) and dun (hill). It was Svindune in the Domesday Book and Swinedon in 1205. Subsidiary settlements, later covered by the railway works, were Eastcott, Nethercott and Westcott and Even Swindon. The great employer – the railway – has now been replaced by light engineering and service industries and local government reorganisation has put Swindon at the heart of a new unitary authority. The importance of the railway coachworks can be seen in pub names in and around Swindon such as the **Flag and Whistle** and **Glue Pot**.

A number of once independent settlements have been absorbed into Swindon. **Rodbourne Cheney** means the reed stream and the name is linked to that of a 13th century landholder. **Hurst Farm** contains the Saxon word hyrst (wooded hill). **Haydon** derives from the Saxon words heg (hay) and dun (hill). It is possible that the first element was gehaeg (hedge). The name is first recorded in 1242 as Haydon. **Haydon Wick** links the name with the Saxon word wic (dairy farm). This presumably was a subsidiary settlement of Haydon. **Moredon** is from the Saxon words mor (marshland) dun (hill) and first appears in a charter from 943 when it was spelled Mordun.

Stratton St Margaret means settlement on the street (Roman road) and this is linked to the patron saint of the village church. The **Rat-trap** pub here – called this since at least 1875 – takes its name from a legendary landlord who locked customers in until they settled accounts on pay day. **Dockle Farm** means the hill where dock grows. **Penn Hill** takes its name from the Welsh word pen, meaning top in the sense of hill. **Kingsdown** was a very recognisable Kingesdon in 1277 and means the hill belonging to the king's royal manor here. **Slade Keys** contains the Saxon word slaed (short valley).

Other place-names in the immediate vicinity of Swindon include **Walcot**, which means cottage of the Welsh and **Okus**, a corruption of oak-tree.

·· T ··

❀ TEFFONT (EWYAS and MAGNA)

This is a very unusual name for two very pretty villages. The name was first recorded in 860 as Tefunte. Its meaning is probably the water-channel on the boundary, from the Saxon word teo (derived from teon, meaning to draw, or demarcate) and funta. There was an Old Frisian word tia, meaning boundary. Funta may be a survival into Anglo-Saxon times of a Latin word fontana (water channel). It may have been borrowed by the first Anglo-Saxon settlers in the area from the indigenous British population . Ewyas is from the barons of Ewyas in Herefordshire who were medieval landowners. Magna means large.

The **Black Horse** pub at Teffont Magna became an inn when the turnpike road was built here in the 1820s, though earlier (in the 18th century) it had been a farm. Curiously an inn with an identical name once stood on the old road to Dinton; this is now a house.

❊ TIDCOMBE

This means either Titta's short, broad valley, from the Saxon name Titta and cumb (a Saxon word for a specific valley shape), or the first element may be the bird name tit, from a Saxon word related to Middle English 'tite'. The name was Titicome in the Domesday Book, Titecumbe in 1197 and Tidecombe in 1249. The church is noteworthy for having no pulpit but possessing a font which may be Saxon. Near the village of Tidcombe is a long barrow which is 56m long and badly damaged by a trench dug along it. In 1750 it was wrecked by treasure seekers.

Nearby **Hippenscombe** – a Saxon name – may be derived from Hyppa's short, broad valley but it is uncertain.

Oakhill Wood was Ocholt in 1259 and comes from a Saxon name acholt, meaning oak wood. The Saxon word holt was often used of a wood in which a single species of tree predominated. The word 'wood' was clearly added when the original meaning was no longer understood. Now the name means literally oak wood wood!

❊ TIDWORTH, NORTH

This was Todeworde in the Domesday Book, Tudeworda in 1270 and Northodesworth in 1313. It means Tuda's homestead, from a Saxon personal name, and worth. South Tidworth is just over the county border in Hampshire. Tidworth is now a garrison town and military history has provided it with street-names linked to the Middle East and the Indian subcontinent such as **Bazaar Road**, **Naini Tal Road** and **Meerut Road**.

❊ TILSHEAD

The name of this village – with its many chequer pattern flint and stone built houses – means Tidwulf's hide, from a Saxon personal name and the word hida. This is clear from the Domesday Book version: Tidulfhide. A hide was a small land holding. By 1403 it became Tyleshide and Tyleshed in 1502. The 19th century stained glass windows in the parish church of St Thomas of Canterbury were home-made in the vicarage. **Flood Cottages** were built in 1842 to replace houses lost in a great flood in the previous year, caused by melting snow.

Copehill Farm takes its name from the Middle English word coppe (rounded hill). Both **Kill Barrow** and **White Barrow** take their names from burial mounds in the vicinity. White Barrow was called Whiteburgh in 1348 and measures 78m long. **The Island** takes its name from a moated house that stood here.

Tilshead Old Ditch is the name given to what is probably the longest long barrow in England. It measures 120m long and is 30m wide and 3.4m high. It was dug into in 1802 and again in 1865. Five burials were discovered. One of the bodies – that of a woman – revealed the cause of death to be most likely a blow to the skull, and she may have been sacrificed to accompany another female burial.

❧ TISBURY

Called Tissebiri, as early as 759, the name means Tissi's fort and contains the Saxon word burg. In an earlier letter of St Boniface it is referred to as Tyssesburg. South-west of the main village is a deserted medieval settlement called Wyck, which would have taken its name from the Saxon word wic (dairy farm).

Apshill Farm refers to aspen trees growing near the settlement. **Billhay** is derived from the Saxon, Billa's leah (clearing).

Castle Ditches is the name of an Iron Age hillfort to the south-east of the village. It encloses some 10ha within triple banks and ditches. It overlooks the valley of the river Nadder.

Chicksgrove does in fact contain the Middle English word chicke (a shortening of chicken). **Farnell** is a shortened version of the Saxon original fearnhyll (fern hill).

Haredene Wood does indeed contain a reference to hares and combines it with the Saxon word denu (large valley). Both **East** and **West Hatch** contain the Saxon word haecce, meaning a gate into a wood. **Linley** is the lime tree leah (clearing); though the Saxon word leah may be used in its older sense of 'wood'. **Tuckingmill** refers to the practice of thickening, or fulling, cloth here.

✖ TOCKENHAM

This is Tocca's settlement, from the Saxon word ham. This is one of the few definite uses of the word ham in Wiltshire. The usual Saxon word for 'settlement' here was tun, which was used in place-name forming from the 7th century and was more popular in western England; ham being more common in eastern England. The name was Tockenham as early as 854.

Tockenham Wick adds the Saxon word wic (dairy farm) to the name of the more dominant settlement. Clearly Tockenham Wick was a daughter settlement of Tockenham.

✖ TOLLARD ROYAL

Simply Tollard at the time of the compilation of the Domesday Book in 1086, it was Tollard Ryall by 1535. The original name is made up of a combination of two Welsh words, twll (hole) and ard (high up). The name probably meant something like pitted hill. The addition of Royal to the name is due to the fact that King John held land here, while he was Earl of Gloucester and prior to ascending the throne in 1199.

Ashgrove appears to explain itself as the ash tree grove. However, while the second element is indeed derived from the Saxon word graf (copse of limited size and managed), the 955 spelling, erse grafan, shows that the first element is not the name of a tree. Rather, it appears to be the name for a part of the human anatomy! It is almost certainly the Saxon word ears (arse) and probably refers to the shape of the land on which the grove grew.

✖ TROWBRIDGE

The county town of Wiltshire and a prominent textile centre from the Middle Ages, its name means wooden bridge, from the Saxon treow (tree) and brycg (bridge). The name appears as Trobrigge in 1184. Trowbridge once had its own castle, but nothing of this now remains, except for the curving shape of **Fore Street** and the name of **Castle Street**. Within the Shires shopping centre is an excellent museum which charts the history of the town with particular reference to its textile past.

In the churchyard of St James's church is a fine marble tomb where Thomas Hilliker is buried. He was a shearman employed in the town's woollen manufacturing, arrested in 1802 and charged with attacking properties belonging to clothiers who were replacing manual labour with shearing machines. Hilliker was hanged in 1803. It was later asserted that he was innocent but knew who the guilty men were; however he would not betray them and so went to his death. The tomb was paid for later in the 19th century by other cloth workers.

Trowle, listed in the Domesday Book as Trole, is probably derived from a stream name, Trull. It now survives as **Trowle Bridge** and **Trowle Common**. **Cock Hill** may contain an unrecorded Saxon word for hill, as it is a common name in England. **Innox Road** – and before it Innox Mill – are from a medieval word meaning land temporarily cultivated. **Conigre** takes its name from the medieval word for a rabbit warren, while **Timbrell Street** preserves the name of Thomas Timbrell who was lord of the manor in 1807. **Studley Green** and **Upper Studley** derive from the Saxon name stod (horse) leah (clearing). **Wyke Farm** and **Wyke Road** have their origins in the Saxon word wic (dairy farm). **Silver Street** has carried this name since at least 1773. **Adcroft** was Addecrofte in the 15th century; the word croft refers to a piece of enclosed land often used for tillage, or pasture. **Holbrook Lane** is ultimately derived from the Saxon name Holebrok, recorded in 1341. It means the stream where holly grows. The small river that flows through the town is the **Biss**. It is a Welsh river name which was probably originally the Bissi, meaning the twig and referring to a tributary stream (in this case of the nearby river **Avon**).

Not all names in the town are so ancient. The **White Horse Business Park**, on the Westbury Road, takes its name from the closeness of the Westbury White Horse. The names of the roads on the park continue the equine theme: **Aintree Avenue**, **Epsom Road**, **Sandown Centre**.

❈ UPAVON

Recorded as Oppavrene in the Domesday Book and Uphavene in 1176 the name means the settlement up the river Avon. This is a Welsh river-name meaning quite simply river. The **Antelope** pub was first mentioned in 1609 but was rebuilt in the 18th century. Nearby Widdington Farm was the birthplace in 1773 of Henry 'Orator' Hunt, a famous early 19th century Radical politician. From Upavon a number of minor roads lead to a series of attractive, quiet villages which lie along the banks of the river Avon and repay exploration.

Bake Barn contains a word found in a number of minor-names in Wiltshire. Originally the word was 'beak'. This is a dialect word referring to land broken up as part of reclamation. Alternatively, it is perhaps possible that in some cases the word was used to refer to the shape of a feature.

Casterley is probably from a Saxon original meaning (wild) cat fort. Local legend claims that a golden chair is buried here. A similar legend is attached to the round barrow at nearby Ensford. Whether these represent two separate traditions, or one that has been duplicated is not known.

The name of **College Farm** is due to the fact that it was owned by King's College, Cambridge. **Town End** is probably so named to indicate a settlement some distance from the heart of the parish.

Widdington was Wydyndene in 1331 and this and other early spellings show that the name does not contain the Saxon word tun (settlement) as might first appear. Instead the final element is the Saxon word denu (large valley) but by the 18th century this had been corrupted to appear as Weddington. The first element is the Saxon word for withies.

✵ UPTON LOVELL

Ubbantun in 957, the name is Saxon for Ubba's settlement. Lovell is from William Lovell who owned the manor here in 1428. The font in the church is Norman but at some time was buried in a local farmyard before being discovered and restored in the 1890s. The church also has a fine brass of a priest, dating from the early 15th century, the stone effigy of John, Lord Lovel, who died in 1408 and the royal coat of arms of George I.

The **Prince Leopold** pub takes its name from Queen Victoria's fourth son.

Golden Barrow is named from a local legend which claims that a man wearing golden armour is buried here. This is one of a number of Wiltshire legends which associate burial mounds with hidden treasure of various kinds. Interestingly in this particular case excavation at Golden Barrow unearthed gold plate, gold and amber beads and a cup. The question is whether the legend pre- or post-dates the discovery. It is hard to tell.

Quebec Barn is one of the many minor places named from distant parts to suggest its place on the edge of the parish.

❋ UPTON SCUDAMORE

This was plain Uptun in 990. It means the high tun (settlement). Scudamore is from Godfrey Escudamore who owned the manor shortly after 1150. The new name appears in the form Upton Squydemor in 1275. The village name is apt as the settlement is perched high above the surrounding countryside, with fine views.

Clear Wood possibly takes its name from a French word meaning glade, to which the explanatory English word glade has been added. Perhaps the Welsh word claear (bright) has survived here but it is difficult to be sure.

Norridge is the north hricg (ridge). It was Northrigge in 1203 which shows the meaning very clearly. The same name also appears in **Norridge Wood**.

Thoulstone – meaning Tholf's tun (settlement) – was first recorded in 1257 as Tholveston. It lies to one side of the busy A36 Bath–Warminster road and is now the site of a golf club.

❋ URCHFONT

This was Ierchesfonte in the Domesday Book, though it had assumed a more familiar spelling of Urchesfunte by 1289. It possibly means Eohric's water-channel, from a Saxon personal name and a Saxon word borrowed from Latin, funta. (See **Teffont**, **Fonthill**, **Fovant**.) The church of St Michael has fine table tombs in its graveyard. The building has noteworthy buttresses and a barrel-vaulted porch.

Crookwood Farm probably contains the Welsh word cruc (hill, mound). **Eastcott** means the eastern cottages and is a Saxon name. In 1167 the name appeared in the form Estcota. **Goosehole Plantation** was Goosehill in 1840. **Oakfrith Wood** was Okfrygh in 1460 and takes its name from the Saxon word fyrhthe (wooded country, land overgrown with scrub).

Redhorn Hill was originally Red Hone and this in turn is a corruption of the Saxon word han (stone). This must have been some kind of boundary stone and such markers – along with other noteworthy features – are used on Saxon charters to outline the boundaries of estates.

Wedhampton was spelled exactly this way in the 13th century and means the weed overgrown haematun (village of the people). **Wickham** is from a Saxon original wicham, meaning in this case something like the dwelling place, the homestead. Research on the compound has suggested that many wichams were settlements close to Romano-British ones. This is because wic was a loan-word from Latin and ham an early Anglo-Saxon word for settlement/village. When compounded they suggest something like 'the Saxon village by the Romano-British vicus (settlement)'. Whether this is the case in all examples is a matter of debate but this should be considered when the meaning of a wicham place-name is being discussed.

•• W ••

WANBOROUGH

This Saxon name probably means waggon hill, from two words, waegn and beorg. Beorg can also mean burial mound. The first element could possibly be wen (tumour) referring to the shape of the hill. It was Wenbeorgan in a charter of 854 and later went through a number of forms including: Wamberga (1091), Wanbrow (1553) and Wonborough (1685). The church of St Andrew is unusual in having both a tower and a spire. It shares this peculiarity with Purton.

College Farm takes its name from Magdalen College, once owners of the land here. An unattractive origin of nearby **Harpit** is apparent from the 1249 spelling, Horput. It means dirty pit.

Kitehill refers to the once common bird of prey which has now vanished from English skies. **Nythe** means marshy ground and is derived from a Saxon word related to isle.

❧ WARDOUR

Close to the site of the fine ruin of **Old Wardour Castle** the settlement takes its name from the Saxon weardora, meaning the lookout hill. It was Weardora in 901, Werdore in the Domesday Book and Wardere in 1461.

Bridzor Farm is Saxon for Brydi's geard (enclosure). **Dunworth** derives from the Saxon name Dunna's worth (homestead). **Haygrove** is from two Saxon words, gehaeg (hedge) and graf (copse of limited size and managed). **Hazeldon** also comes from two Saxon words. The first is obviously the hazel tree, the second is denu (large valley).

Totterdale is the lookout hill where deer are found. In the 12th century it was Totederehilla. All the elements in the place-name are Saxon.

A fascinating example of how very minor names can have an ancient history is provided by **Twelve Acre Copse**. A charter of 984 refers to this area of land as 'be twelf Aceron'. The name has survived for more than a millennium.

Wallmead is an interesting survival and probably means in Saxon the maed (meadow) of the Welsh. The Saxon word for the indigenous people of Britain was wealh, meaning foreigner and from this the English word Wales/Welsh is derived. However, later in the Anglo-Saxon period the word was also used generally of slaves, so it is not always possible to be absolutely sure of the cultural characteristics of the people so described. Nevertheless since many in the latter category would have been Welsh, the problem of definition is not great.

❧ WARMINSTER

This handsome market town, now also a garrison town, was first recorded as Worgemynster in 901. The name means the minster-church on the (river) Were, from the Saxon name of the river (which means the wanderer) and the Saxon word mynster. A minster was an early church which served a wide area. Like many such churches the minster at Warminster was sited at the centre of a royal estate of the rulers of Wessex. The antiquity of the town is reflected in its street names. **Chapel Street** and **West Street** are first recorded in the 14th century, while **Church Street** was Churchewey in 1581 and **Portway** was called Newport in 1360. The earliest record is that for **High Street**, first mentioned by name in 1279. The town is now home to a number of army activities, including the School of Infantry and workshops of the REME.

Arn Hill probably derives from the Saxon word aern (house), though there is the possibility that another Saxon word – earna (eagles) – may underlie the name of this now wooded hill. **Kidnappers' Hole** behind clearly refers to some now lost local legend or event.

Battlesbury Hill actually contains the Saxon personal name Paettel. The Iron Age hillfort encloses 10ha and has two ramparts separated by a ditch. There is also a large inner quarry ditch. It is possible that a medieval motte was constructed within the fort and this may explain the mound on the south-west. Quarrying outside the north-west entrance unearthed a mass grave and this may be from the Roman conquest of the area, or from some unrecorded tribal warfare.

Boreham is another Saxon name meaning the farm belonging to the burg (defended settlement); a reference to Warminster.

Bishopstrow means the bishop's tree and legend has it that when St Aldhelm preached here his ashwood staff sprouted. In the 12th century it was called Biscepes truue.

Bugley is also a Saxon name and means the bug (goblin) leah (clearing). **Cop Heap** derives from the Saxon word copp, meaning top. This is obviously a reference to its height which is clearly seen from the town. It is a distinctive hill.

Henfords Marsh is the marsh frequented by wild fowl. **Sambourne** is called Sandeborne in a record dating from 1249 and is Saxon, meaning the sand burna (stream).

Smallbrook Meadows, now a conservation area, is first referred to as Smalebroke in 1275. It is an alternative name for the river Were from which the town is named.

Woodcock Road takes its name from Woodcock Farm, mentioned in 1840. On the road is **Kingdown School**, the town's comprehensive school, whose badge – the red dragon of Wessex – commemorates the fact that the town was a royal estate of the rulers of Wessex.

❧ WESTBURY

Famous for its nearby White Horse and cement factory chimney, the town was Westberie in the Domesday Book. The name is Saxon and means west fort, from its position below a prehistoric hillfort (**Bratton Castle**) on the western edge of the highland of Salisbury Plain. **Chantry Lane** is first recorded in the 19th century as Little Chantry and refers to land belonging to Salisbury Cathedral. **Maristow Street** means literally 'Mary's place' and again refers to land belonging to the Cathedral church of St Mary, Salisbury. **West End**, in the town, was Weststrete in 1375. **The Butts** is a reference to where archery was practised in the Middle Ages. The modern method of theme-naming is clearly seen in housing estates with clusters of names such as **Elm -**, **Ash -**, **Cedar -**, **Lilac -**, **Hazel -**, **Chesnut -**, **Beech -**, **Willow -**, **Sycamore -**, **Hawthorn Grove**. Elsewhere there are **Dorset Drive**, **Wiltshire Way**, **Hampshire Gardens**, **Somerset Drive**. These are very typical of this modern trend.

Beggar's Knoll probably refers to unproductive land and is of the same type of name as Starveall, etc. **Bridewell** is literally the spring of the brides. It was Brudewelle in 1341. It may refer to some local belief in the spring enhancing fertility.

Frogmore is the mere (pond) where frogs are found. **Redland** is probably derived from the Saxon word hreod (reeds), referring to marshy land.

Westbury Leigh takes its name from the Saxon word leah (wood, or clearing). In 1242 it was simply Lia but was later expanded to give a clearer picture of its location. In 1302 it was Lye juxta Westbir and in 1581 it had developed into Westbury Leyghe.

❧ WESTWOOD

The name has changed little from Westwuda (987) and its meaning is obvious. The present sub-divisions of the village into **Upper** and **Lower**

Westwood are of long standing and are reflected in 14th century references to Overwestwode and Nether Westwode.

Avoncliff takes its name from the river and the steep sides of the valley. In 1590 it was called Ancles Weers, referring to the weirs of fulling mills located here. The Kennet and Avon Canal crosses the river and the railway here via an aqueduct.

Lye Green is from the Saxon word leah – clearing in woodland. Earlier in the Anglo-Saxon period the word had meant wood.

❀ WHITEPARISH

The 1301 spelling – Whiteparosse – shows the meaning as white parish, derived from the Middle English word parosse. The second element has replaced an earlier one as in 1278 the place was called Whytechyrche.

Abbotstone was Abbedeston in 1249 and means the tun (settlement) belonging to the abbess; in this case the Abbess of Wilton.

Alderstone Farm was first recorded in 1166 and is named from an otherwise unknown Saxon called Ealdred. **Blaxwell** was Blakeswell in 1242 – Blacer's wiell (spring) in Saxon.

Brickworth has changed considerably in spelling since 1255 when it was Brycore. It is derived from a Welsh word brig (summit) and a Saxon word ora (hill-slope, foot of a slope). **Cowesfield House** is named after a certain Cufel and was Colesfeld in the Domesday Book.

Mean Wood is actually derived from gemaere (boundary). **Whelpley** was Welplega and is Saxon for the leah (clearing) of the hwelp (cubs).

❀ WILCOT

In 940 this was Wilcotum, though by the time of the compilation of the Domesday Book in 1086 it had contracted to Wilcote. It means in Saxon the wiell (spring) cotum (cottages).

A 19th century excavation of a disc barrow by **Gopher Wood** turned up an urn, an incense cup, an awl and a bone pin. A line of seven other barrows extends north from this barrow. These other burial mounds are all bowl barrows.

Oare was Oran in 934. It comes from the Saxon word ora (hill-slope, foot of a slope). Nearby is the **Giant's Grave**. This is not actually a burial mound but the remains of a promontory fort. According to local legend the giant will come out if a person runs round the site seven times.

Rainscombe does not refer to the weather as it might first appear but to the raven's short, broad valley, from the Saxon words hraefnes and cumb.

Stowell is the stan (stone) wiell (spring) in Saxon.

❧ WILSFORD

This was Wiflesford in the Domesday Book and Wylesford in 1279. It means the ford belonging to a Saxon named Wifel. **Ham** contains the Saxon word hamm (land in a river bend).

Nearby **Lake** is derived from the Saxon word lacu (small, often slow moving, stream). Located here is one of the important barrow cemeteries found around Stonehenge. This one consists of at least 15 bowl barrows. In addition there are four bell barrows, two disc and a long barrow, the oldest dating from the New Stone Age, while the other burial mounds date from the Bronze Age. Among others, at nearby **Lake Down** is yet another barrow cemetery consisting of 16 different kinds of Bronze Age round barrow. This great concentration of burial mounds indicates the importance of the area around Stonehenge in the Bronze Age.

Normanton seems to mean the tun (settlement) of the northmen and was first recorded in 1332 with an identical spelling to that of the modern place. On **Normanton Down** there is what has been called possibly the most important Bronze Age barrow cemetery in England. There are some 25 round barrows of various types and two long barrows. In the **Bush Barrow** an extended skeleton of a man was discovered in 1808, along with three bronze daggers, a stone mace, an axe, a shield and a lozenge shaped sheet of gold.

Rox Hill is a corruption of rook's hill. In 1227 it was Rockeshulle. **The**

Sling takes its name from a narrow strip of woodland and the reference is probably to a thin thong of leather. **Starveall** is a fairly common reference to unproductive land, also found elsewhere in Wiltshire.

❧ WILTON

Synonymous with excellent carpets, the name has changed little since 854 when it was spelled Wiltun. It means Wylye settlement, from an abbreviated form of the river-name and the Saxon word tun. **Kingsbury** and **South Street** are all first recorded in the 13th century. **Minster Street** refers to the Benedictine nunnery here and was Munstre in 1348. **Silver Street** probably indicates that silver smithing occurred here. **Crow Lane** was originally Crawellane in 1494 and means the crow-spring lane. The county name **Wiltshire** is the area of land with Wilton as its chief town. Originally Wiltshire was Wiltonshire.

Bulbridge means, as it appears, bull bridge. It was first recorded in about 1200 as Bulebrige.

Ditchampton is a Saxon name meaning the tun (settlement) of the people living by the ditch. The reference is to **Grim's Ditch** which runs through Grovely Wood. This too is a Saxon name, the dic (dyke/ditch) of grimm (the masked one). This was an alternative name for the pagan god Woden. There are Grim's Ditches in Hertfordshire, Middlesex and Oxfordshire. However, the Wiltshire one is the first to have been recorded and was mentioned as early as 956.

Washern is first recorded in the Domesday Book as Waisel. In 1307 it was spelled Washerne and this suggests that it comes from the Saxon word aern (house) and means the wash house. It is close to the river Nadder and the name may refer to a place where sheep were cleaned.

❧ WINGFIELD

This is Wine's open country, derived from a Saxon original, winefeld. The first element may be the Saxon word winn, used in the sense of pasture. In 954 the name was spelled Wuntfeld, though Domesday Book gives a clearer spelling: Winefel. Saxton's map of the 1570s preserves the spelling Winfeld. Sometimes known as Winkfield, the intruding 'k' is first recorded in 1535 and also occurs in later records. **The Poplars** public house stands near the main road; part of it was a farmhouse in the 18th century.

Midway Manor is between Wingfield and Bradford on Avon. It was the home of Henry Shrapnel, who in 1803 invented the shrapnel bomb, and bombs surmount the gateposts that stand on the Bradford road.

The farmstead of **Pomeroy** dates from at least 1001 when it was Pumberig and is derived from a Saxon name, plumbyrig (plumtree fort).

Snarlton contains the Saxon word tun (settlement) but the first element is obscure, which makes it impossible to be sure of the overall meaning of the place-name. **Stowford** was originally stanford in 987, meaning stony ford (across the river Frome).

Swansbrook was Swinbroch in 1001 and means the burna (stream) of the pigs. Usually the Saxon word for streams in the clay country is broc, but this is an exception.

Rowley – site of a deserted village – means rough clearing. Nearby was the settlement of Wittenham, the location of which is also lost.

❧ WINSLEY

This was Winesleg, in 1242, its meaning is Wine's leah (clearing) and it is a Saxon name.

Conkwell probably takes its name from that of the nearby steep hill. This must have been called cunuc, a British name; ancestor of Welsh.

Danes Hill has no connection with Vikings but instead takes its name from the Danys family who lived here in the 16th century. The same name is found in **Dane Bottom**, though this appeared as Dean Bottom in 1840.

Hartley was Hortleye in 1289 and means the leah (clearing) frequented by harts (deer). **Haugh** is derived from the Saxon word haga. This meant enclosure or hedge. **Turleigh** is not derived from Saxon leah (clearing) but from the Saxon word thyrelung (piercing), a reference to the steep valley. **Ashley**, as it appears, is from the Saxon ascleah (ashtree clearing).

❊ WINTERBOURNE (BASSETT and MONKTON)

Just plain Winterburnan in 964, the name means stream that flows in winter. Bassett is from Alan Basset who owned the manor in 1220. Monkton is from the Abbey of Bocherville, France, owners of the manor in 1114. The large number of Winterbournes in the county arise from chalk streams subject to summer drought. The Saxon word 'burna' was used to describe clear streams, whilst the word 'broc' (modern brook) tended to be used to describe muddier waters.

Near **Winterbourne Bassett** is **Rabson** which takes its name from an abbreviation of the tun (settlement) of the abbess. In 1242 it was Abbedeston but by 1275 the shift to Rabbedeston had started. From here the name shortened to Robston by 1544 and to Rabson by 1719. It is an example of how a place-name can change dramatically over time and how the change can totally obscure the original meaning of the place-name.

Richardson looks like a familiar surname but in fact in 1242 it was Ricardeston and means the tun (settlement) of Richard. It is an example of the way in which the Saxon word 'tun' was used in place-name formation for some time after the Norman Conquest.

Near **Winterbourne Monkton** is **Hackpen Hill**. This takes its name from a combination of the Saxon word haca (hook) and the Welsh word pen (head, hill). The name means a hook-shaped hill. It was hacan penne in a charter dating from 939.

Windmill Hill is the site of the largest New Stone Age causewayed camp in England. It covers 8.5ha and excavations have discovered over 1,300 pots, flint and stone objects and animal bones. Many were buried in the ditches and have been radio carbon dated to about 3350 BC.

❊ WINTERBOURNE (DAUNTSEY, EARLS, and GUNNER)

Again these were plain Wintreburne in the Domesday Book. The name Dauntsey is from Roger Daunteseye who owned the manor in 1242. Earls is from the earls of Salisbury, owners by 1198. Gunner is from Gunnora de la Mare, landowner in 1250.

Near **Winterbourne Dauntsey** is **Figsbury Ring**. This is an Iron Age hillfort and it may contain the Saxon word fugol (wild bird). However in 1695 it was Frippesbury and this may suggest that the first element was in fact the Saxon word frithian (defensive) corrupted into 'fripp'. In the 18th century it was also known as Clorus' Camp but this is clearly an antiquarian invention designed to link it to the Roman invasion of Britain. The fort is enclosed by a bank which is 3.4m high surrounding an area which covers 6ha. Excavations in the mid 1920s suggested that an early structure lay within the fort, revealed by another ditch but no bank. This may have been either a New Stone Age causewayed camp, a henge monument, a quarry ditch, a stock enclosure or a line of defence which was never completed. Bronze Age and early Iron Age pottery have been recovered from the site.

Near **Winterbourne Earls** is **Hurdcott** which derives from the Saxon for the cottage of the herdsmen. In the Domesday Book it was Herdicote.

❧ WINTERBOURNE STOKE

This was Wintreburne Stoch in the Domesday Book. The second element is derived from the Saxon word stoc, meaning outlying farm. In 1325 it appeared as Wynterbourne juxta Chitterne.

The Coniger was Conyngarclose in 1466 and means rabbit warren. In the Middle Ages rabbits were an important source of fresh meat in the winter.

King Barrow is so called because excavations here produced valuable artifacts. **Scotland Farm**, as with so many of this name, refers to a fairly distant site. It is first mentioned in 1773.

❧ WINTERSLOW

Called Wintreslev in the Domesday Book the name is Saxon and means the hlaew (burial mound) of a man named Winter. A local legend claims that a golden coffin is buried in the vicinity of Winterslow. This is a fairly common legend and found associated with a number of places in Wiltshire.

The Pheasant pub was the scene of an amazing event in 1816 when an escaped lioness attacked the London–Exeter mailcoach here. Surprisingly the horse, which was the subject of this attack, survived.

Hound Wood, as the name suggests, is the wood of the hunting dogs. In 1275 it was Hundewude. **Middle Winterslow** was Wynterslewe Middelton and means middle settlement from a Saxon original, middeltun.

✳ WOODFALLS

This was Wudefolde in 1258 and comes from two Saxon words, fald (fold) and wudu (wood). In 1508 it was Wudfoldshutte in which the name was extended with the addition of the word sceat (corner). This is another Saxon word.

Kite Croft reveals the presence of the bird of prey which was once extremely common in England.

✳ WOOTTON BASSETT

The meaning here is wood settlement, from two Saxon words wudu and tun. It was Wdetun in 680, Wodeton in the Domesday Book and a more recognisable Wutton in 1229. Bassett is from Alan Basset who owned the manor in 1230. **Stoneover Lane** takes its name from a nearby field, which in the 1840s was called Stoneover Mead. **Sally Pussy's Inn** actually recalls a former landlady, Sarah Pursey.

Bishop Fowley demonstrates the way in which the appearance of a name can seriously alter its apparent meaning. This is actually a corruption of a Saxon name which was either fugolhyll (wild bird hill), or fulhyll (foul hill). The first word is not bishop but probably a Saxon byxegehaeg (boxtree hedge).

Vastern is probably derived from the Saxon word faestaern (stronghold). **Woodshaw** is derived from the Saxon word sceaga (copse, underwood on the edge of a field).

Wootton Bassett Town Hall

🌸 WOOTTON RIVERS

This derives from two Saxon words, wudu (wood) and tun (settlement).
It was Wdutun in 804 and Otone in the Domesday Book. It had gained
its surname by 1428 when it was Otone Ryver. This comes from the name
of Walter de Riperia, who owned land here in 1212. The church of St
Andrew is famous for its clock which dates from 1911. This clock is constructed from pieces donated by visitors and has letters instead of numbers. In addition it has a different chime for every quarter hour, for six
hours.

Flitwick probably means the wic where flicce (flitches of bacon) were
produced. In this example the Saxon word 'wic' is used of a subsidiary
settlement without the meaning of dairy farm.

🌸 WORTON

In 1173 this was Wrton and it means the herb settlement from two Saxon words, wyrt (herb, kitchen vegetable) and tun (settlement). By 1195 the spelling had become Wurton and by 1622 Woorton.

Hurst takes its name from the Saxon word hyrst (wooded hill). **Littlecourt** is derived from the Saxon for little cottage, with the second element cot, not court. **Lutseye** is probably the ieg (island, land bounded by water) belonging to Lutt.

✾ WRAXHALL, NORTH

This form is very different from the Domesday Book spelling: Werocheshalle. The meaning is possibly hollow frequented by birds of prey, from the Saxon words wroc (which may have referred to such birds) and halh.

Mountain Bower is actually a corruption of Monkton's Bower and refers to Church land here.

Sheepsleight Wood derives from the Saxon word slaeget, meaning sheep pasture.

✾ WRAXHALL, SOUTH

Situated north of Bradford on Avon, this village was Wrokeshal in 1242 and probably has the same meaning as North Wraxhall. The two compass references tell the villages apart. It first appears as Suthwroxhall in 1468.

Chesland Wood may contain the Saxon word cisel (gravel), referring to soil quality. There is a possibility that the Middle English word cheste (conflict) is involved in the forming of the name. If this is so then it might suggest some form of land dispute took place here.

Norbin takes its name from the Saxon words north binnan (north within), which suggests that although it is in the north of the parish, it is still included in the parish. **Norton Barton** probably refers to a beretun, a farm where barley and other cereals were stored.

❧ WROUGHTON

Spelled Wervetone in the Domesday Book, this is the tun (settlement) on the river Worfe (a lost river-name). The settlement had an alternative name which first appeared in 890 as Ellendun – eldertree hill. As late as 1620 this dual name occasionally appeared; in this year it was called Wroughton alias Elingdon. A battle was fought here in 825 between the West Saxons and the Mercians and, according to the *Anglo-Saxon Chronicle*, 'great slaughter was made there'. The battle was a West Saxon victory.

The **Brown Jack** pub commemorates a racehorse which won the Alexandra Stakes at Ascot in six successive years, between the world wars.

The hillfort of **Barbury Castle** takes its name from two Saxon words that mean Bera's fort. It was the site of a Dark Age battle in 556, when the West Saxon ruler Ceawlin defeated the British here. The fort itself dates from the Iron Age and encloses 4.7ha. It is strongly defended by two banks and ditches and there is some evidence to suggest that the ramparts were faced with sarsen stones. A barbican was constructed to protect the more accessible eastern entrance. Aerial photography has located hut circles and storage pits within the fort. Excavations in the 19th century discovered Iron Age tools, weapons, harnesses and chariot fittings.

Blackgrove is from the Saxon for black graf (copse of managed woodland).

Chilton was spelled exactly this way when it was first recorded in 1245. It probably means the young people's settlement from the two Saxon words cild (child) and tun (settlement). In names such as this the word 'child' is probably used of a young retainer rather than a little child.

Elcombe is the elder-tree cumb (short, broad valley). **Ladder Hill**, also called Ladder Lane, or Egg Lane, takes its name from a local custom of rolling eggs down it on Good Friday.

Quidhampton was Quedanton in 1196 and means the cwead (dung) haematun (settlement of the people). The same Saxon name is found near **Bemerton**.

Salthrop means the salt sieve, from the Saxon words sealt hearpe. Quite why such a tool was associated with this place is unclear.

❉ WYLYE

This is a place-name taken from a Welsh river-name, meaning the tricky river, a reference to flooding. The place-name first appeared as Biwilig in 901. Later variants include Wilgi (Domesday Book), Wily (1199) and Wely Abbatissa (1502). The last name arose because the Abbess of Wilton held land here. **Nettlemead Lane**, in the village, takes its name from a field called Nettelmeade as early as 1570.
The strangely named **The Bake** probably refers to the shape of a local landscape feature, as in 1840 it was called Beake.

Nearby **Deptford** means the deep ford. It was Depeford in the Domesday Book, Duppeford in 1281 and Debtford in 1630.

❉ YATESBURY

Recorded as Etesberie in the Domesday Book, it possibly means fort with a gate, from two Saxon words geat (gate) and burg (fort). Alternatively, the first element may be the Saxon name Eata. If the meaning is the former it may suggest that in the Anglo-Saxon period the old fort was re-used either in a defensive manner, or as an animal holding area. This might explain why the reference to 'gate' was thought significant. It is hard to be sure in a case like this and either could be possible. The name was Hyatebir in 1199 but had developed into Yatebury by 1297. The 800 year old church rests on sarsen stones, of the type used to build Avebury and Stonehenge.

Little London is on the edge of the village and may be a comic reference to distance. There are a number of names of this type in Wiltshire where distance is measured by naming the area from some far off place.

Stert Pond is derived from the Saxon word steort. This meant tail, or tongue shape and clearly describes the shape of this particular landscape feature.

Vulpit probably means wolf pit and may have been some form of trap. Alternatively the first element may be Wolf used as a personal name but this does not seem so persuasive when coupled with the word 'pit'.

❧ YATTON KEYNELL

Plain Getone in the Domesday Book, the name means settlement in a pass, from the Saxon words geat (meaning pass, rather than gate, in this instance) and tun. Keynell is from Henricus Caynel who owned the manor in 1242. The form Yatton Kaynel first appears in 1289. In 1530 the village was called Churcheyatton but this name did not survive.

Broomfield means, as the name suggests, that this was the open country in which broom grew. The word field may be derived from the Saxon word feld (open country) or it may represent the later use of the word for an area of enclosed land. The first element in Broomfield may explain the meaning of **Broom's Farm**, a little to the south-west. Alternatively this may represent a local family name which gave rise to a minor place-name.

Folly Farm may refer to land with a disappointing yield and it is a fairly common minor name in Wiltshire.

Nearby **Giddeahall** was Giddy Hall in 1773, though its meaning is obscure. It may well be some kind of joke, or even a form of reproach. The original reason for the coining of this name remains unknown.

Grove Farm may contain the Saxon word graf (grove, copse), but the name need not be ancient as the word has continued into modern usage.

Kent's Bottom takes its name from a family living in the parish in the 18th century. **Long Dean** derives from the Saxon langdenu (long and large valley). In 1422 it was le Longdene. **West Yatton** was first differentiated by name in 1279. It is actually south-west of Yatton Keynell.

··Z··

❧ ZEALS

This, the only Wiltshire place-name beginning with a 'z', was actually spelled Sela in the Domesday Book. The name means the sallows, or willow trees, from the Saxon word sealas (plural form of sealh). Zeals is on the edge of the old forest of Selwood, the name of which had the same derivation. The 'z' spelling first appears in 1637, in the form Zailes. Following the English Civil War, the landowner here, Colonel Penruddock, led a Royalist uprising in 1655. For this he was executed.

Wolferton was Wolfertun in 1219 and Wolverton in 1327. It is a Saxon name and means the tun (settlement) of Wulfhere.

Castle Grounds Farm takes its name from Jocelin de Castello who owned the land here in 1257. Whether the castle was in the vicinity and gave rise to the surname or whether the surname was taken from a castle elsewhere is not clear.

The Green has been called this since at least 1327 when it gave its name to the landowner, John atte Grene. This surname means literally 'at Green', 'living at Green'. The name itself is almost certainly derived from Saxon gren (green) and may describe a particularly attractive piece of land.

Nor Wood, recorded in 1257 as Nortwud, is the north wood. **Zeals St Martin** takes its name from the dedication of the parish church.

ACKNOWLEDGEMENTS

I am very grateful to a number of people for their help in the preparation of this book: Muriel Hodgson for the line drawings; Mike Marshman (Wiltshire Local Studies Librarian); Dr B. Millett (of the University of Southampton) and Margaret Gelling (of the University of Birmingham) for advice; my mother and father for their encouragement. My greatest thanks are to my wife, Christine and our daughters, Hannah and Esther, for their unfailing interest, love and support.

All royalties from this book will be donated to the charity National Strategy for the Advancement of Rural Women in Uganda (NSARWU).

BIBLIOGRAPHY

Below are listed publications for those wishing to study the origins of Wiltshire place-names further. EPNS stands for the English Place-Name Society. Where my own interpretations concur with the derivations offered in these studies, I am indebted to the depth of scholarship of these other researchers. Often, however, I have decided between different previous suggestions, or offered my own derivations, or definitions of words used. For errors I alone take full and undivided responsibility.

Davey, C. **West Country Place-names** (1985)
Ekblom, E. **The Place-names of Wiltshire** (1917)
Ekwall, E. **The Concise Oxford Dictionary of English Place-names** (4ed,1960)
EPNS **Place-names of Wiltshire** (1939)
Gelling, M. **Place-names in the Landscape** (1984)
Jones, M, Dillon, P. **Dialect in Wiltshire** (1987)
Longstaff, J.C. **Notes on Wiltshire Names, Vol. I. Place-Names** (1911)
Tomkins, R. **Wiltshire Place-names** (1983)

INDEX

This index only includes major place-names; it does not cover the roads, streets and public house names.